What others are saying...

"An up-close and personal look into the lives of some of the most "high risk" children in America. This is a story of one family's journey as Christ leads them into His will for their lives....ministering to the children of the incarcerated...the forgotten children...the ostracized children...who through no fault of their own suffer bullying, shame and very often feeling abandoned. Well written, powerful and convicting. It will challenge all who read it into searching their hearts to see how to get involved. A must read for those in ministry or those with children...one of these children most probably goes to your child's school."
Bobby McGee, Director
ChristSong Ministry

"Grace and Ben Smith are a truly amazing couple, who have dedicated their lives to helping "the least of these," those invisible victims of the crimes of their parents. Grace's account of their journey is told with grace, mercy, and compassion for both parent and child."
Debbie Walsh, US Director of Prison Ministry
Child Evangelism Fellowship

"What a wonderful story of one special couple following God's lead to reach out to kids that have fallen through the cracks of broken families and neglect. Have your tissues ready as you read the heartwarming stories of how God became the father to the fatherless and the hope to the hopeless as children discover the love of God through Camp David of the Ozarks. Be encouraged and challenged to follow God's leading in your own life as Ben and Grace responded to God's call to rally others to "follow their dream" of helping children of prisoners to rise above their own difficult circumstances and use God's love and power to impact others for His Kingdom."
David Jaquess, Executive Director
New Life Ranch

"The statistics are alarming. The vast majority of inmates' kids end up in prison themselves. Does anyone care? Benjamin and Grace Smith do and they are making a difference in the lives of some of America's most at-risk kids. Dream with them, dream big. And trust God to make these dreams come true, not only for you but for the kids whose very lives depend on it."
Fauhn Schierer, Executive Director
COPE - Coalition of Prison Evangelists

Grace Smith
Prov 3:5-6

Shame is No Longer

my name.

The journey of one couple to reach some of the most at-risk kids in America

Written by Grace Smith

For Camp David of the Ozarks'
10 year Anniversary Celebration

This book is dedicated to the man whom I have
shared this dream and journey with,
Benjamin A. Smith
I would never have attempted a book had you not
always said, "Someday we'll write a book"
I admire your faith, your care for people, and
your optimism. You are my inspiration and the one
who helps keep my focus on our Father God,
who makes all this possible.

The purpose of this book...

- To inspire others to step out and follow their dreams
- To encourage others to trust in God's provision and care
- To raise awareness about some of America's most at-risk children and youth, and how to give them hope

Note: All of the stories in "Shame is no longer my name" are true. Most of the names of the children in this book have been changed to protect their privacy.

Writers: I have shared many articles and stories that my husband Ben has written and published in our Camp David Newsletters over the years. I wove his stories of the campers together with the story of our journey, and shared some of my favorite camper stories too. I also included, with permission, several stories from our staff and some testimonies.

Permission was obtained to use the song lyrics, stories, testimonies, and photos.

Table of Contents ᎒ᐟᔦ

Acknowledgements

I want to give thanks and praise to God for whispering, "*Write a Book!*" in my heart and leading me each step of the way. I have felt His incredible love as I wrote about our journey, and He has provided in ways that completely exceeded what I thought possible. I know this is His message that He wants shared.

So thankful for my love, Benjamin, who has shared his stories from camp and helped edit this book. As I was writing our story, there were times I just didn't feel like I could finish, but he kept encouraging me and telling me I could do it.

Very grateful to Laura Valenti, who was the first person I told that I was going to write a book, and she has been the best cheerleader and coach as I wrote!

Thank you, Uncle Larry Stone and Geoff Stone, for your professional advice and help.

Thanks to Rachel, our Office Manager, who did the photo shoot for the book covers and to Laura Marchbank, for helping with the graphic design on the cover.

A huge thank you to those who helped to edit the book: Cindy Smith, Carol Hudler, Sandy Schmid, Beverly Flori, Kathy Collins and Heather Buller. You put a lot of time into editing (grammar is not my strong point!), and I am so very grateful. Thank you for your prayers for this project too!

Foreword

Written by Mary Kay Beard, Founder of Angel Tree

GRACE, one of the most powerful words in the English language, not simply because it is the author's name and my own Mother's name, but primarily because it is God's awesome gift to us: "For it is by (God's) grace we are saved, through faith, and that not of ourselves, lest anyone should boast. It is the gift of God."

The GIFT is first of all our own salvation and secondly, it is the privilege we are given to be instruments of God's Grace. God gave to me the gift that ultimately became Angel Tree. Children of inmates are the first victims of crime and incarceration. They do not choose their parents nor do they have any voice in the choices made by those parents. Yet, overwhelmingly they (nearly 7 of 10), are more likely to become our next generation of incarcerated people.

What will it take for this to change? I believe that exposure to the Body of Christ in early childhood experiences, e.g. VBS and camp, makes a profound and lasting impression on children. I know it did in my life. The earlier the foundation of Love and Truth is laid; the more likely they are to avoid incarceration.

Grace Smith has written authentically and skillfully of the journey she and Ben Smith embarked upon some ten years ago. Camp David of the Ozarks has been "home base" and each "encounter" with the child of an inmate has been an experience that neither they nor the child will forget. In turn the children have experienced God's love through hugs and laughter, good food and games. They have experienced new challenges and how to apply God's Word to these challenges, such as how to control their anger and hurt and how to express gratitude by serving others.

The purpose of Camp David is stated as: giving HOPE, extending GRACE, bestowing VALUE and revealing the FATHER. Grace Smith tells stories about these children which will make you laugh and cry. Your heart will never be the same. These first- hand encounters told by Grace Smith in "Shame is no longer my name" will reveal very clearly that she and Ben are fulfilling the purposes of Camp David of the Ozarks.

Introduction

Written by: Shandia Johnson, Educator and Dean of Character Education at Lighthouse Preparatory Academy

This "Introduction" was written by a mom who sent her sons to camp, and came to serve as staff herself. I believe this perspective from the inside out will prepare your heart to hear the stories in the rest of the book.

It was a beautiful, warm, and sunny afternoon when we stepped off the church van that brought us to the back fifteen acres of a farm near Rolla. From the first moment the doors of the van flung open, cheers and shouts of joy urged us off the van and into the main building while young men in yellow shirts grabbed our luggage and followed close behind. Not long after, another larger van pulled into the circle drive, and we watched as a repeat of our welcome took place. Kids poured off the van with looks of surprise and some seemed a bit bewildered. Within moments everyone was gathered in the main hall where introductions were made, teams were formed, and instructions were given for all the campers to unload their belongings in their assigned cabins or wagons. This was the first day of Camp David in 2013.

Everywhere I turned there were smiling faces, compliments, and kind words. I was overwhelmed by the amount of *happy* that existed here. It was obvious that there was one goal and one focus among the staff: the campers. The staff understood that each of these campers was in need of compassion, a gentle touch, a tender word, and someone to love them right where they were. All of the campers at Camp David are children of prisoners, and my two oldest sons were campers that week.

It had been three years, three months, and fourteen days since that terrifying day that turned our lives completely upside down. It was a scene all too familiar to me from my childhood, only instead of the police arresting my stoned and drunk step-father they were at my current house arresting my husband. Although my step-father would always be back in a few days, my husband wasn't coming back. He was sentenced to eleven years in prison. In the space of a day, I lost my spouse, and my children lost their dad.

My three sons were eight, nine, and twelve, and all of us bawled uncontrollably as I shared with them what happened to their dad. We cried together as I held them and told them that it was okay to cry and okay to feel whatever they were feeling. I told them that it would not be the last time we cried about what had happened, and that crying again would be okay too. It hurt! It hurt worse than a broken bone, or surgery, or a terrible accident. It felt like a death. We grieved like it was a death.

We spent the next two weeks inside our house afraid to go out or return to normal activities unsure of what others would say or how they would treat us. That week's newspaper carried the story of the events of the previous days – our horrifying events - and was followed up by radio coverage of the same. The pain was raw and deep. We were not the ones who committed the crime, but we carried the weight of the shame of the one who did.

As time went on, we tried to adjust to our situation. My children felt out of place at school and were afraid to be honest about where their dad was. At times one of them told the other kids his dad was on vacation or had gone to Alaska. I understood this as I too felt the pressure of not wanting to let others know that he had been arrested. Being a single woman with three children was hard enough without letting others know about the rest of our situation. I felt incredibly vulnerable to judgment, condemnation, and ridicule especially by those who didn't know what it was like to walk in our shoes.

Over the next year, we learned that we could be vulnerable
with those who truly loved us even though it was only a
handful of people. My middle son shared his dad's situation
with his best friend after about a year, and I too shared with
one of my friends. It was nice not to carry the load alone. It
was during this conversation with my friend that I heard the
name Camp David for the first time. She explained that it was
a camp for children of prisoners and that her son volunteered
there every summer because he loves it so much. She
suggested that I should look into it.

Having never heard of a camp like this I was intrigued and
looked it up online. My internet search led to a phone
conversation with the camp secretary who encouraged my
interest. By the time she finished answering my questions, I
not only wanted my sons to attend, but I wanted to go and
help serve. Despite my lack of finances to send them, she
informed me that they could still go. Each year financial gifts
sent to Camp David, by caring and compassionate givers, were
used to sponsor the campers who couldn't afford it
themselves. Because of such generous giving we were going
to camp that summer.

In all honesty, I was a bit nervous about camp, and my boys
were almost reluctant. They didn't know what to expect,
what they were in for, or how they would be treated. After
our first hour or two there, my youngest son came to me and

excitedly whispered in my ear, "Hey Mom, you know how at places there are always mean and crabby people?" I said, "Yeah." He responded enthusiastically, "Well, I haven't seen one around here yet!" In fact, a couple of days later he again assured me that no mean or crabby people existed at Camp David because he had seen some situations where the workers had every right to be grumpy. He was right. I felt as much affected by the genuine love and compassion that was pouring from the workers as he did. Even when a hurting camper acted out, the counselors, leadership, and staff responded with deep compassion and tenderness. Never once did anyone ever raise their voice, glare, or say an unkind word. Love was the one word communicated throughout the camp: through smiles in the lunch line, a gentle word during a difficult moment, a shout of celebration for just being who God made you, a note of encouragement, a helping hand during chores, a look of reassurance that you have value, a quiet moment where someone else listened to your pain, and an environment where you could be you without judgment, condemnation, or shame.

While swinging on the swings at the end of one of our first few nights, my eleven-year-old turned to me and asked with genuine curiosity, "So...everyone here has a parent in prison?" I nodded my head in confirmation, "Yep, that's right, every one of the campers here." "Wow..." he said. His voice trailed off as he pondered the implications. For the first time in almost three and a half years, we could speak freely. It hit me in the kitchen on the second day while I was helping prepare lunch for the campers. One of the cooks and I were discussing our families, and I mentioned that two of my children were campers. Stating that my children were campers automatically meant that their dad was in prison. She didn't flinch. Again when talking with Grandma Pansy, the camp Grandma, I freely shared that my children's father was in prison. I remember feeling shocked that it came out with such ease and no fear of rejection or criticism. I realized that Camp David provided an environment where I felt safe, and with this safety came a freedom previously unknown to me. I knew it wasn't just me that felt this freedom though. Every camper there was affected by it. It was evident in the change in their demeanor and behavior from the first day to the last, their bolstered courage to share their hurts and struggles, and their tears when they left on the last day.

Every one of us – campers and workers alike – felt the freedom of the unconditional love that permeated this camp. I marveled and wondered at this until I met the camp directors, Ben and Grace Smith, and had the opportunity to chat with them. It was evident immediately that there was a supernatural gift of compassion that drove them and the work they started at Camp David. Although they had personally never experienced the devastation of having a family member in prison, they gave credence to each camper's feelings and pain as though they themselves had been pierced by that same pain. Through their depth of compassion and abundance of loving kindness, they unconditionally validated the worth of every individual, and this empathy flowed from Ben and Grace to the rest of the leadership, counselors, and staff. I thank God for these two hearts that heard the call and felt the compassion for children and families like mine!

Chapter 1

That Ain't Right.

We passed the Kleenex box around the table and sat in stunned silence. One of our team members had just shared a story she had recently learned about one of our campers, one of our girls. What had happened in our local elementary school is something no child should have to experience.

This camper, whom we'll call Penny, first came to camp in 2010. We had invited children to come to that week of camp through a local food distribution program. Standing in a gravel parking lot under the hot sun, we watched as parents and kids waited in line with their empty boxes. As we handed out invitations to the parents for their children to come to a free week of camp, we didn't know the turn of events that would take place. Up until that point, Camp David had been a camp solely for children with one or both parents in prison. But our hearts had felt God's tug as we saw many needy children in mobile home parks close to camp, and we knew that offering one week of camp to children in low-income families was a way we could serve our local community.

There were several things that stood out during that first Community Kids' Week. The dining hall was much quieter than it usually was. It was like many of these local kids were just coasting, trying to get through life and "survive." Many of our "regular" campers (the ones with parents in prison) have experienced hardships which caused them to be fighters! Other things stood out in the dining hall—these kids actually said, "Please," and, "Thank you," as they went through the serving line for food. After six weeks of summer camp and rarely ever hearing those words from campers, it was sweetness to our ears! And this group of kids went back to the food line again and again! The cooks were not prepared for the difference in the amounts that the community kids ate and we had to make extra runs to town to buy more food!

The most difficult thing about this week was the kids' homesickness. These kids had never been away from home before, and since their moms lived just minutes from camp, it was easy for them to pick up their kids and take them home. We were unprepared for how quickly the kids could go from laughing during a field game to crying on the phone to mom and begging her to come pick them up. For our regular campers, there are more often tears running down their cheeks because they ***don't*** want to go home on Friday.

But the thing that stood out the most was that this group of kids talked about their dads. They talked about things they liked doing with their dads, what sports their dads liked, etc. It was as if they actually knew their dads. The reason this stood out from all the other weeks of camp is that our regular campers never talk about their dads that way. They don't live with their dads or know when they are going to see them again. Most of them feel totally rejected by their dads, and they don't believe their dads care anything about them. Some are scared out of their wits at the thought of seeing their dads again—after what he did to them or their moms.

This is why we have this little unique camp for children of prisoners—because our kids are fatherless. James 1:27 says, *"Pure religion and undefiled before our God and Father is this, to visit the fatherless and widows in their affliction..."* We believe that the fatherless children in our communities across America are close to God's heart. And as God's people become more aware of the epidemic of fatherlessness that we are experiencing as a nation, more and more are asking, "What can we do to make a difference?" And that is how Camp David exists—caring people wanting to make a difference.

Penny stood out during that first Community Kids' week. She talked about her dad a lot. Penny knew her dad cared about her and loved her. She also made friends with everyone at camp, and she even learned most of their names. I remember watching her walk back from the food line one lunchtime. She stopped at one table after another to give hugs. That little girl with the curly pony tail and cappuccino colored skin was a hugging machine! I think she hugged me at least three times a day!

Many months after camp, we were heartbroken to learn that Penny's dad had sold some bad drugs which ended up killing someone. We learned about what happened through someone else in the community because the story of Penny's dad had made headlines—not because he had won a community service award or had served his country in the army. He was charged with manslaughter. Can you imagine going to school in your small community after your dad was all over the headlines for murder?

Penny didn't come to camp the next summer, but she came again in 2012—only this year we sent her an invitation to come to our regular weeks of camp. She was now not just a child from a low-income family in our community, she was one of "those." "Those" kids whose dads were locked up. "Those" kids whose families were known for their involvement with crime, not church. Penny didn't bounce around like she had two years before. I think I only got one hug from her all week. Her eyes didn't seem to sparkle as much. Maybe I just didn't notice because she avoided eye contact and looked down more than up, but something had changed.

All of these memories came back to me as our team sat in stunned silence around the conference table. One of our new staff members has a daughter in the local school system and had just asked us if we knew a girl named "Penny." We affirmed that yes, she was one of our girls. This staff member went on to tell the story. Recently one of Penny's teachers called attention to Penny in front of her entire class. Apparently Penny had lied again and it hit his button. He decided to do what seemed to us to be one of the meanest things a teacher could ever do. He called Penny up to the front of class and put an inmate picture of her dad up on the big screen so the whole class could see. He told Penny that if she didn't quit lying, then she would end up exactly where her dad was—in prison.

That just ain't right.

What do you think Penny felt as her dad's mug shot was shown to the whole class? Can you imagine what the other kids in Penny's school say to her now as they pass her in the hallway since that teacher shamed her? If anything, her teacher has now given her classmates permission to despise and shame her too. Who will be her friend?

I pondered the teacher's actions and wondered if he felt that shaming a child would somehow stop the cycle of crime in her family. I believe that what that teacher did WILL have effects on that little girl, but probably not the ones he wanted.

16/ That Ain't Right.

I did some research on the effects of shame. I learned that shame makes us feel terrible, like we're horrible people, worthless, and disgusting. Clinically speaking, some common effects from shame are addictive disorders, self-destructive behaviors, and other psychological symptoms such as rage, hostility and bullying. Shame motivates people to withdraw from relationships which brings isolation. Research shows that when shaming has been severe, it can actually contribute to the development of mental illness.

On the other hand, research also shows that the best weapon against shame is **empathy**. When we take time to understand how it might feel for a child to have a parent incarcerated and empathize with their feelings of hopelessness and shame, we can be part of making a significant difference in some of American's most at-risk children.

What if there was a place where Penny could just be herself, a place with empathy and without any shame?

Chapter 2

Not Normal

Our campers never feel "normal" once they experience having
a parent incarcerated. They feel like they are the only ones
who have a parent in prison, and that becomes something
they try to hide in order to be accepted. They feel alone.
Judged. Hopeless.

I never experienced that kind of shame.

My husband and I both grew up in Christian homes and
trusted in Christ at early ages. I think my life was pretty
"normal" for Christian kids in America. My dad was a
computer programmer, my mom was a stay-at-home mom, I
attended a private Christian School, and we went to a large
Baptist church. It was at that church that I first felt the call of
missions on my heart at age 10. But my "normal" had already
started changing in my life at that point—my dad had done a
radical thing and almost ended up in jail for it! He pulled my
brother and me out of school and started homeschooling us!
This was in 1984, and homeschooling was a new movement.
Three years later, my dad made another radical decision, and

sold his share in a family business and moved his family (I am the oldest of nine children, with seven brothers!) to a place out in the country. He wanted to work with his sons in a new family business. Dad was influenced by the conservative homeschool community and some Mennonite friends which resulted in me having to drastically change my wardrobe to a very conservative dress code, including head coverings. My life was anything but "normal" anymore, and I felt alone a lot in my teen years. I did read a lot of missionary biographies, and for my 17th birthday I asked for a Spanish/English Bible as I was studying Spanish. I also bought my own guitar because I really wanted to be ready to serve God, and I was sure Latin America would be part of the plan. But over the next two years my parents' focus in the home became more and more "family" centered and, as I tried to honor them, my dream of being a missionary began slipping away.

One unique thing about my family- while many parents encourage their children to compete in sports, spelling bees or music competitions, my dad was always thinking of new business endeavors for my brothers and me. At age 11, my younger brothers and I ran a snack business in the offices where my dad worked. At age 14, I was boarding horses in my dad's barn and making a profit at it. By the time I graduated from high school, I had a specialty sewing business and had three ladies who sewed for me. When I look back over my life, I see how my dad's entrepreneurial spirit influenced the wild adventure I jumped into later in life. When it came to trying something new business-wise, my dad had a *"You can do it!"* mentality. My dad also taught us kids to work hard. Life wasn't easy in a big family living on a farm, but I would have never attempted the things God had planned for me if I had been afraid of hard work.

It was through our local homeschool group that I met Benjamin and his family. They weren't really "normal," either. They always had foster children with special needs staying with them and usually a lonely adult or two that needed the love of a family to help them figure out where they were going on their journey. When we met at age 14, Ben had already gone on his first mission trip—a three month adventure with Teen Missions to the country of Greece. Ben's parents were all into missions (that's what they did for "family vacations!") and serving God in radical ways. In fact, they were in the process of adopting a 13-year-old boy from El Salvador. Over time, Ben became like one of my brothers. He came out to my family's farm every chance he got! My dad included Ben in the family projects and taught him how to pour concrete and drive the backhoe. He also taught Ben to not be afraid to try new things. Ben was interested in learning to butcher, so after he put his first two deer in the freezer, my dad put him to work on our family bull!

As young teens, Ben and I liked each other. Our homeschool group had monthly roller skating get-togethers, and Ben and I would skate together or chase each other in a game of "tag"! Then we heard a teaching about saving our teen years for the Lord and not playing the dating game, and we tried ignoring each other for several years. Every time I turned around, Ben was off on another mission trip (he's been in 16 different countries). After a while I resigned myself to the fact that he would probably fall in love with a girl he'd meet in Africa or Russia.

At age 20, Ben spent almost a year in Moscow, teaching English in the public schools and working with juvenile delinquents. In the fall of 1995, he returned to the US and moved back in with his parents. He began seeking God's will for his next step, and asked his parents for counsel, too. After considering several options, it was suggested that it was time for Ben to find a wife and get married.

You know, when you grow up with someone, it's easy to take them for granted. While Ben hadn't fallen in love overseas, he still had an idea of how he was going to find "Mrs. Right," and I wasn't in the picture. But he was trying to be wise about this whole marriage thing, so he thought he'd make a list of what he was looking for in a girl. As he came to the end of his list, it hit him that I was a perfect match! As Ben sought the Lord in prayer about developing a relationship with me, God gave him a verse, *"Hath not God chosen the poor of this world to be rich in faith, and heirs of the kingdom which he hath promised to them that love him?"(James 2:5)* Writing this verse now, I am impressed with the promise and hope that verse had! Ben and I could have never stepped out and done the crazy things we've done if God had not made us rich in what was really important- faith. Our faith didn't come of ourselves. It came from our strong Christian roots, and reading many biographies of great missionaries. They were our heroes.

With my dad's approval, Ben and I started courting, spending most of our time with each other's families. Since I had known Ben for six years already, I knew he had an adventurous spirit and a caring heart. While on dates, I loved learning more of his deeper thoughts about life, and what was important to him. A big thing that knitted our hearts together was a passion to serve God in ministry—of course we were **sure** that was overseas missions! I was so excited that God had opened a door for me to follow my dream of being a missionary. Three weeks after we started courting, on January 20, 1996, Benjamin proposed during a special dinner he had planned. I responded with an excited, "Yes!" He had become my best friend in that short time, and I was in love! As we prepared for our wedding, friends asked what we needed for wedding gifts. What kind of wedding gifts do you need when you are planning to be missionaries overseas? Suitcases!

We were married on June 8, 1996, with almost 200 guests in attendance. During our wedding ceremony we sang a song together that was written by Ron Hamilton:

"Lord, send us anywhere, Only go with us;
Lay any burden on us, Only sustain us.
Sever any tie, Save the tie that binds us to Thy heart—
Lord Jesus, our King,
we consecrate our lives, Lord, to Thee."

Less than three weeks from our wedding day we went to our first "anywhere" together—a mission trip to Mexico with Ben's church!

But the words in the song, *"lay any burden on us, only sustain us,"* would be tested many times on our journey together.

Ben and I were married on June, 8, 1996

Chapter 3

Shut it Down

Did you ever have a dream, and put yourself 100 percent into following it, only to have it turn out differently than you thought? Sometimes as Christians we think that since we are going to serve God, everything will work out great. I learned that wasn't true early in our marriage.

It was as a young married couple, expecting our first baby, that we encountered our first big, "That Ain't Right." The story unfolded in a little town about an hour south of Guatemala City.

It had already been a bit of a journey to get to that city. As Ben and I set up our first home, we would talk for hours on end about when we would work as missionaries with a specific organization—picturing ourselves helping on a mission base in deepest Africa. Then the moment came when we were sitting at the dining room table filling out the paperwork to go to the first training this mission organization offered. Some requirements came up in the paperwork, and we suddenly realized that we didn't have peace about continuing to fill it out. I'll share more about that-in a later chapter. It wasn't that we suddenly didn't want to be missionaries. We just knew it wasn't going to be with that organization. But it threw us into a feeling of uncertainty and seeking God. Within the next month, we miscarried our first baby and totaled our first car in a snow storm. Grief was added to the uncertainty. As we sought God in prayer, we asked an older missionary that was in the states for counsel. She encouraged us to go to another country together for about three months and do at least a month of language school so we could see what that was like before making a huge commitment to a mission organization. Several months later, Ben's cousin Brad, who was a missionary in Guatemala, invited us to come down and help in an orphanage there. We felt immediately that this was what God wanted us to do. After months of planning and saving (and discovering that we were going to have another baby), we packed up the suitcases we had gotten as wedding gifts, and embarked on our first big mission trip together.

I loved the small orphanage with 20 kids, and busied myself with helping to pat out corn tortillas, cleaning the big house, and my favorite, fixing the girls hair! Ben helped in the big garden and loved playing soccer and cops and robbers with the boys. After a month of helping there, we moved into Guatemala City to attend language school. One weekend we took the bus back down to the orphanage to visit, and that's when some things started to not line up. During that month, the orphanage director and his family were in the states trying to raise more support for their ministry. Through a strange turn of events some former orphanage staff shared some things with us that we had not known previously about the orphanage director. He was a Guatemalan man married to an American woman. What we hadn't known earlier was that this man had worked in another orphan ministry and had been caught abusing the girls in that facility. As the seriousness of that situation sank in, we became very concerned about the fact that he had girls in this orphanage. It was also odd to us that two of the girls that had been there had suddenly left. When the missionary returned from the states, we met with him and shared our concern about his past and asked him to consider going to counseling. We also shared our concern about him "ministering" to girls at all. He admitted to the story from his past, but insisted that he was a forgiven and changed man. We explained that we felt we could not stay if he didn't get counseling. So with heavy hearts, we left the orphanage. We really didn't know where to go as we weren't supposed to fly home for another month! When we got to the big city, we called a pastor we had met there, and he told us we needed to get over to his office right away. As we sat there in the little office, our hearts broke as the pastor told us that the grandma of one of the girls who had recently left the orphanage had just reported to him that the orphanage director had been visiting the girls' rooms at night and sexually abusing them. When I realized I had been living on the other end of that facility when that horrible abuse was going on, I was sick to my stomach. We ended up staying with missionaries in the city and trying to do everything we knew to do to get the rest of the children out of that orphanage. The story only got worse as it was uncovered. Sadly, the other missionaries discouraged us from taking the matter to the civil authorities, but we did all we could to rescue the kids. When we returned to the states a gentleman that had been on the board of directors for that orphanage contacted us and asked Ben to compose a letter relating the facts of what had happened and his concerns. The letter was then sent to all the supporters of that ministry.

My innocent little world was shattered. My fantasy of being a "missionary" now came crashing down. Instead of God opening doors for us to be missionaries in Guatemala, He had put us in a situation where we had to stand up for kids that were being abused. Instead of helping the orphanage to be successful, we had to help shut it down because it was **unsafe.** How could things like this happen?

That Ain't Right.

Chapter 4

God's Whisper

Our first baby was born just over a month after we returned
from Guatemala. It was a welcome distraction from the
sadness I felt from our experiences there. Bethany Grace was
actually born at our home on her due date! In the months
following her birth, my parents encouraged us to move to
Missouri and build a home on their land. You see, after Ben
and I got married in 1996, my family moved from York,
Pennsylvania to the Missouri Ozarks. They wanted more land
and freedom, and to live near a growing home church group.
Now my dad was offering Ben and me land to build on, as
he wanted to give a portion of his property to each of his
children. We thought it was the best thing we could do at that
point. We had been renting half a farmhouse in Lancaster,
Pennsylvania, but that brought a lot of complications when
we were gone for that three-month mission trip! Looking
forward, we assumed God must have more short-term
mission trips planned for us so we jumped at the chance to
build. Ben was excited about the idea of living in a rural
setting; with turkeys and turtles crossing the roads and lots of

deer in the woods. I liked the idea of living close to my family, and quickly learned to appreciate all the native wildflowers that grew alongside the gravel roads in Missouri. I did NOT like all the dust that came from those gravel roads!

A problem arose after we moved. We were now 18 hours away from Ben's family, and they missed their little granddaughter. They solved that problem within a year by moving just five miles from my family! I know it is unusual for both sets of grandparents to live within five miles of a young family, but it gets even more unusual. Five years later Ben's grandparents moved from Pennsylvania to Missouri, and his family built onto their home so they could care for their elderly parents. They ended up with three generations living on the same farm!

Our home during that first year in Missouri was a 10-foot-wide (skinny!) blue mobile home at the top of my parents' land. When Dad and Mom Smith bought their 55-acre piece of land just a few miles away, Ben decided to fix up a little old house on their land for us to live in. I actually told Ben it couldn't be done when I first saw the house. It had last been used as a greenhouse, a carpenter's shop, a dump for all the previous owner's junk, and, of all things, a chicken coop!! There was a THICK layer of chicken manure all over what would have been the living room and two bedrooms! To make this scenario even more disheartening to me as a woman, the bathroom had dead chickens in it when we first looked at it! But feeling there were no other good options, I came alongside Ben and we started remodeling that place. Our church family even came out and helped us with the project! Ben had started his own remodeling business, so he'd work on that house in-between jobs. That fall our second daughter, Esther Joy, was born in our "new," but unfinished home. It was a difficult birth and I hemorrhaged badly. I almost went unconscious, but we cried out to God and over the next hour my blood pressure came back up and stabilized. I was so thankful to have both our families close by as I recovered from the birth. Little Esther was a good baby, and Bethany adored her baby sister.

Our curly haired Bethany, and baby Esther

I enjoyed being a stay-at-home mom to our two darling blue-eyed little girls. Ben's remodeling business was growing, and his dad even began working with him on jobs. But while Ben was away at work all day, every day, the desire to serve God in ministry began to burn again in my heart. We had both become busy with life, and it had been awhile since we had talked as a couple about ministry. One summer day as I was cleaning, the thought came, "Maybe God hasn't opened doors for us on the mission field, but he must have something for us to do." That night I shared my thoughts with Ben, and proposed that we begin praying each day for God to show us His next plan for our lives.

A month later, as I was walking back to our house from the barn, I looked across the green valley behind Ben's parents' barn. In that moment it was as though God whispered, "CAMP." I went into the house and with the girls playing in the living room, I began washing the dishes and thought about the word "camp." My pulse began to race and excitement began to build to the point I couldn't hold it in, so I called Ben at work. "Ben," I softly ventured, "I was outside looking across the valley and I think God gave me the word *camp*. What do you think that means?"

Ben took a moment to ponder the idea. Then I heard his enthusiastic response, "We should start a camp!" Suddenly, it was as though we both thought the same thought, at the same time. "This has to be a camp for troubled kids." Wow. It was a huge, crazy idea. Way bigger than us. But not bigger than our God.

God gave us the word "camp" in 2000, but we had no idea how we were going to start a camp. We knew we needed to pray and, since the vision included Ben's parents' land, we talked to them a lot about it, too. They prayed with us and were excited about the idea. I got a notebook and started writing ideas down. I found a listing of camps across America, and called to ask them to send me their brochures. I cut those brochures all up and glued the things that I liked to my notebook. I took that notebook with me when we went back to Pennsylvania to visit relatives, and they were excited for us. My Aunt Kathy still mentions that time when we showed them that little notebook with our dream.

God led us to an organization called, "Christian Camp and Conference Association," which we joined, even though we didn't have a camp yet. It was the best thing we could have done. The association was having an annual camp conference in Oklahoma, and Ben decided we would go. We had just found out we were expecting baby number three, and I was very sick with morning sickness. By the time we reached New Life Ranch in Oklahoma, I was so sick from those winding roads that I wanted a new life myself! When I was finally able to get off my bunk bed and walk to the chapel, I was greeted by warm smiles and a spirit of love and acceptance by everyone. I was shocked how this group of people from different church backgrounds and denominational camps could all come together and share their passion for God and kids. I had never experienced anything like it. I had seen church groups divide over many different issues and interpretations in the Bible. Being in a large group of believers who were united in their focus of serving God and kids was like a glass of ice-cold water. I wanted to join this community of camping ministers and be part of this new family.

Sometime around then we learned about an organization called "Royal Family Kids' Camps" that worked with churches to provide camps for children in foster care. They had this little blue book full of stories about abused and neglected kids that would come to camp and have life-changing experiences. I read it over and over again. I loved all the special things they did for the foster kids: a two-campers to one-counselor ratio, camp grandparents who would write the campers letters, and a birthday party for everyone. They would even send the campers home with a special photo album of pictures of themselves at camp— "to keep their happy memories alive" the booklet said.

Ben and I were so excited about the idea of doing Royal Family Kid's Camps with our church. It would cost $500 to go to the first training at a Royal Family Kid's Camp, and we carefully saved the money to go. But there was one more requirement before we could start the training. Royal Family required a team of people from a church to go. We had to have a treasurer and one other person join our team. Our pastors allowed us to share our vision for doing this kind of camp, and we appealed to our church family to join us in this new adventure. But we didn't have enough people step forward. Everyone was very busy in their work and lives. We prayed and prayed and talked to lots of people. But the training time came and went for two years, and we still didn't have enough people to begin. It was very discouraging.

What we didn't realize was that God was training and preparing us all along. He sent us three troubled youth to whom we opened our home. One situation involved a young lady's dad entrusting her to us so we could "make" her see that he was right. Sadly, we instead learned about abuse in the home and had to fly to her hometown to help her mom get the children to safe housing while she reported the dad. Another young lady was actually one of the orphans from that orphanage in Guatemala! Anna and her sisters had been adopted by a friend of mine. Due to the severity of the trauma and abuse they had experienced early in life, she and her sisters had to be separated. The hope was that they could find healing and bond with caring adults. Anna lived in our home for over a year and we learned a lot about helping kids with attachment issues. Now Anna is happily married and is a wonderful mama to her own little girl. Those years of waiting for God's big plan were not wasted; He was training and preparing us. We got a lot of practice in **standing up for hurting kids and reaching out to them with love and grace.**

Chapter 5

Sick As Dogs

During that two-year period of trying to start a Royal Family Kids' Camp, God sent us a baby boy! Number three was birthed in a plastic swimming pool in our living room, my best birth and biggest—10 lbs, 8 oz!! We named our boy after Ben's brother and dad: Timothy Daniel. I got Timmy's two big sisters new baby dolls when he was born so they could care for their babies while I cared for "mine." While we were busy changing diapers and feeding babies, we learned about a mission project that needed help in Guatemala, and I wanted to go. Feeling discouraged from trying to step out and follow God and things not working out, plus that old desire for adventure and serving God as "real missionaries," made it seem to me like the perfect time to go. I knew if we were going to start a camp, this would probably be our last opportunity to get out of the country. I was still holding onto a dream that we were going to serve overseas, rather than living forever in the rural Ozarks. I really wanted to pack those suitcases again.

Ben became excited about going and helping with the building project—something he was good at. He thought it would be a great experience for our three kids to be in another culture and see how other people lived. This time when we talked to people at our church about going with us on a three-week trip, we had five people jump at the opportunity. In no time we had a team of ten people (including our kids ages 5, 3, and 10 months) that were heading to Guatemala with Ben and me as team leaders. This was in the summer of 2003 when Ben and I were 28 years old.

Our project was to build a concrete house for a blind man and minister to the people of Alta Verapaz. They spoke Poqomchi, a language that was in the process of being written down for the first time. One memory stands out from all the rest. Our host missionaries (Ben's cousin!) wanted to take us two hours into the mountains to preach in one of the little villages. As Ben drove the rented van along those winding paths, we passed village after village

Visiting a village 4 hours north of Guatemala City with our three children.

with thousands of people living in them. NOT ONE of those people could read because their language was just being written down. NOT ONE of those ladies or children we passed on the road had ever seen a Bible. That hit me so hard. All of them were lost—without hope.

As I remember that trip now, I think of the campers and prisoners' families living in inner-city St. Louis and rural Missouri that we have met over the past years. I've talked with moms who can't read; which presents a problem when I ask them to fill out a registration form for their child. We've had campers who can't read and have no one to tutor them. And even though they live in America— the land of opportunity—when a child comes to our camp, it is often the first time he has ever held a Bible. They don't know about David and Goliath and Daniel in the lion's den. These American kids, just like those people way up in the mountains of Guatemala, are without hope.

While in Alta Verapaz, we visited with a family who were translators with Wycliffe Bible Translators, and it was exciting to learn about their work to translate the New Testament into Poqomch. Their home was up on a hill and overlooked part of the village to which they were reaching out. I remember looking out over the field below us and watching children play soccer and wondering if God was going to open the door for us to return there and build a camp. But He didn't (at least not yet)! No one invited us to come back, and it felt to Ben like everything was just closed doors for future ministry there. We finished our building project and headed back to the states with our team and kids.

When we got home, I tried to settle back into a routine with my kids and get caught up on laundry, but I didn't feel good. I started to wonder if I was experiencing morning sickness again. But it just kept getting worse, and after two days I couldn't even get out of bed. We were both scared. I had never vomited that much with morning sickness nor had I been so weak. With concern written all over his face, Ben carried me out to the van, drove to town, and carried me into the doctor's office. As our doctor listened, his face grew concerned too. He asked a lot of questions about our time in Guatemala. Did we get any vaccines before we went? NO. Because we were not doing a *medical* missions trip, the missionary told us not to worry about getting vaccines. Did we eat any food that was prepared with unwashed hands? Probably. My tired mind went back to that chicken foot soup we had eaten in that little hut with the dirt floor shortly before we had left the country. There had been no running water near that house. Where was the doctor going with these questions? Then I heard a scary word. Hepatitis.

I was sent over to the hospital for more blood work which confirmed the doctor's fears. I had Hepatitis A, which is contracted by eating food that was prepared with contaminated, unwashed hands. The worst part was that there was nothing the doctor could do for me at that point. I had to let the virus run its course in my body. Thankfully, we were able to take our children to get booster shots and they never got it. But several days after I got sick, my dear hubby got sick too. Our skin actually turned yellowish, and so did the whites of our eyes. The vomiting went away after five intense days, but I was so weak. It was six weeks before I could walk out of my house and drive to town. I remember vividly the day I managed to walk across the yard to my neighbor's house. It felt like I had walked five miles. We were blessed to have family that lived close, and they took such good care of us and our kids.

Ben was concerned as he carried the weight of not being able to work and provide for his family during his weeks of recovery. Not only had we used all our savings to purchase our plane tickets to Guatemala, but after taking off work for those three weeks, now all he could do was lay on the couch, too weak to even help with laundry.

We were right where God wanted us. He had not left us. He provided for all our needs those weeks. And He kept bringing to Ben's mind that word that He had spoken two years previously to us—CAMP. Lying in bed one day, the thought occurred to Ben, *"We aren't going to get any closer to starting a camp until we step out and start doing it."* With that thought in mind, Ben decided, as far as it lay within him, we would have our first weeks of camp during the summer of 2004. The more he thought about camp, the more excited he became. Camp seemed like a perfect match for us as a couple. It encompassed many of the things we enjoyed. We both loved to create special events. Ben was a builder. I liked to make things beautiful. We were both visionaries, and we both loved working with kids.

As Ben thought about camp, he remembered working at a little camp in Pennsylvania when he was a young man. *"I remembered my first summer as a counselor. I was 16 and I had four boys in my cabin, and I made a lot of mistakes. I gave almost all the boys in my wagon wedgies. For some reason, that is what I thought the cool counselors did! The camp director was very patient with me as he sent a camper to tell me, 'no more wedgies!' When I absolutely couldn't get my boys to sleep, the director poked his head in and yelled at the boys, and they were silent after that. The thing that I enjoyed most about camp was being included with the rest of the staff. I was quiet and had a hard time fitting in with my peers. It was that week **I had the privilege of leading one of my campers to Christ and that left a huge impression on me."***

Through the CCCA organization, we had learned about the incredible impact Christian Camping can have. Going to a

Christian camp for one week can impact kids more than going to Sunday School every Sunday for a year. There is just something about getting kids out of their normal surroundings, and out into nature, where they can laugh and play with caring adults and connect with God. Now imagine kids coming to camp that have <u>never been</u> to Sunday School in their entire lives. Camp can be <u>life changing</u> for them. Another fact that impressed us was the large percentage of pastors and missionaries that had given their lives to God and dedicated themselves to full-time service, at a summer camp. We became convinced that camp ministry was something worth investing ourselves in.

As we lay on our living room couches, as sick as dogs, we talked. And talked. And dreamed together. We remembered a couple that we had met at our last camping conference, Cliff and Susie Johnson. The Johnson's had started a camp for children of prisoners seven years earlier. They shared stories about prisoners' kids so excited about God that they were reading their Bibles at night in their sleeping bags by flashlight. (These kids had never seen a Bible before in their life!) Another story was about a time when they were sharing the plan of salvation and had asked, "Do you know what sin is?" A kid raised his hand and responded, "It's the fun stuff we get to do!" These were the kinds of kids we wanted to have come to our camp!

Chapter 6

Giant Killers

When young David heard the Philistine giant tearing his
people down with his degrading comments and blaspheming
his God, he decided to do something about it. He tried to go
before the giant with the king's armor on, but it just didn't fit
him. Then David decided to just be himself, and with a heart
full of faith, he walked out into that battlefield with just his
sling and some little stones. He had a 9-foot-tall giant to kill,
and with God's help, he was going to do it. We had our own
kind of giant we were facing. We wanted to start a camp for
kids that were being shamed and rejected in our society, but it
was very daunting to think of starting our own camp. So many
questions tumbled about in our heads: *"How do you start a
camp? What do you need? How will we raise funds?"* It was
hard to know which stone to pick up and throw first.

God provided many answers to our questions through this
very special couple, Cliff and Susie Johnson. Remembering
them from our camping conference earlier that year, we
called and asked if we could come for a visit. I was still very

weak from the Hepatitis A virus, but Ben was doing better by then. He drove the entire family on the three-hour trip to Sagrada Scholarship Bible Camp. After taking us on a tour of their camp, they invited us into their home where we began asking tons of questions. Cliff and Susie had developed their camp from the ground up, and were serving about 250 children of prisoners each summer. The moment that stands out to me during our visit was when Cliff said, **"Ben, you can do it. Susie and I started with nothing and we built a camp, and you can too!!!"** That was exactly what we needed to hear. We needed someone to believe in our dream enough to say, "You can do it!!" Cliff and Susie shared everything from their camp rules and how they set up their 501(c)(3) organization, to the building plans for a covered-wagon cabin and the reason behind having separate boys' and girls' weeks. They excitedly shared all they could, because they had been praying for years for more camps like theirs to start!!

We left the Johnsons' home and camp so full of inspiration. Not only were we inspired about starting a camp for children of prisoners, but their family inspired us. I'll tell you more about that later, but we were even more sure we wanted to be involved with camp ministry when we left that day.

The first BIG need in starting a camp, was provided by Ben's parents, Dan and Cindy. They were the first ones to hear our dream and believe in it. They very generously offered the use of 10 acres of their property, which they later donated, to this dream. Through lots of hard work and living on less than half an acre of land in eastern Pennsylvania, Dan and Cindy had been able to save up and purchase 55 acres of land in Rolla, Missouri, debt free. So when they offered to donate land, it was a precious gift. Not only

did Dan and Cindy believe in our wild dream of camp, they stepped out in faith and started a prayer ministry for hurting people called, Shepherd's Heart Ministries.

Land— a precious gift from Ben's parent's Dan & Cindy Smith

Choosing a name for the new camp was a very weighty decision. We had spent the past two years dreaming about starting a camp and trying out different names, but now was the time for a decision. A lot of camps include something about their landscape in their name, such as *Camp Cedar Cliff* or *Lakeside Bible Camp*. Others named their camps after a person or character quality, such as *Camp Hope*.

After much prayer, we choose the name *Camp David of the Ozarks*. When we say, "Camp David," people often get a puzzled look and ask, "*You mean, like the place for the president? Isn't that in Maryland?*" Actually, we weren't thinking about the president when we chose the name. We were thinking of a scrawny little boy who was left in the fields to take care of sheep, who became a "Giant Slayer."

This Bible character named David was the youngest of seven brothers. No one, not his dad, his brothers or even the prophet, expected David to amount to much. This is similar to the plight of children of prisoners. They are EXPECTED to fail. However, through the hardships he faced, David put his faith in God and became one of the greatest kings of Israel. David was known throughout history as a man after God's own heart.

This was our dream for the children that would come to our camp: that the most at-risk children in America would become giant slayers. The giants that prisoners' children face are huge and intimidating. But we know, like David, they CAN overcome, and they CAN become men and women after God's own heart.

Chapter 7

Holding Up Our Arms

Now that we had land and a name for our camp, we began sharing our dream with everyone. But it was a pretty preposterous plan. We were a young couple with three little ones, still in our 20's, and we had no savings. We hardly had any camping experience and no college education because it wasn't encouraged in our families growing up. What we did have was a library of missionary stories that gave us faith that God could do big things with willing hearts.

Not everyone in our community agreed. A common comeback was, "*Why don't you just use another campground and rent it for your program?*" The problem is that every campground we phoned in the local area booked their own programs in the SUMMER and were unavailable when we needed it! Comments like: "*It's so risky,*" "*You need more land,*" or "*You should wait until you are 30 years old to start because that's how old Jesus was when he started his ministry,*" came from well-meaning people in the community. The hardest response came from some family members. They felt camp could never make an impact on troubled youth unless we required all our female staff to wear head coverings and dresses. They also felt the urban youth that came to camp needed to be taught conservative standards of dress. We had followed these convictions ourselves for many years. Now as we sought the Lord on this matter, He reminded us of some of our heroes. Men like Hudson Taylor, who went against the norm for missionaries and dressed like the Chinese that he was trying to reach with the Good News. We didn't want "dress" to come in the way of campers meeting their Father God. It was very hard, though, to deal with this family criticism. It really hurt when I went to family gatherings and these family members would turn their backs and walk away as we shared our stories, pictures and excitement about what God was doing at camp. I had to keep going to God, asking Him to help me to forgive. It was four and a half years before these family members had a change of heart and were willing to visit the camp for the first time—even though they lived close by. What a joy it was that day when I was able to give them a tour of the camp and show them what God was doing at this little camp with a big heart.

When we step out and start doing what God has led us to do, sometimes those closest to us will oppose us. Ephesians 6:12 states, "*For our struggle is not against flesh and blood, but against the rulers, against the authorities, against the powers of this dark world and against the spiritual forces of evil in the heavenly realms.*" I really don't think the enemy of our souls wants there to be special programs or camps for troubled kids. I believe he targets people that stand up for those little ones. What better way to discourage us than to turn family members, whom we love, against us. How grateful we were that there was a group of mighty men and women that surrounded us and held up our arms as this spiritual battle was going on.

The doctor who treated us when we came back from the mission trip with Hepatitis A not only agreed to be a board member, but he and his wife donated their 24-foot round above-ground pool to the camp. That is still the same pool we are using today, ten years later! The youth leaders at our church believed in our dream and agreed to be on the board of directors. The husband was also co-president of an engineering firm and his expertise was such a blessing with all the construction that has happened at camp over the years. My best friend's husband, who was good with finances, became our treasurer. A university professor and his wife, who I considered my spiritual mom and dad, supported us a lot with prayer. I was pleased when the professor agreed to become a board member. Dad and Mom Smith were also board members; in fact, the organization was formed as "Shepherd's Heart Ministries," with Camp David being a branch under their 501(c)(3). At that point, Shepherd's Heart was much bigger than Camp David, and we weren't sure how fast the camp would grow. I think the board was surprised when, just two years later, the camp had grown to the point where we needed to separate the two ministries. Camp David became its' own 501(c)(3) organization.

The first board meeting took place on November 17, 2003. At that point we had a board of directors, 10 acres of land, a pool, and a list of friends and family to whom we could send a newsletter. Here is an email newsletter that we sent out that winter:

Camp David News

Vol. 1 Number 4   **January 2004**

Welcome to *Camp David News*! This is a monthly e-mail newsletter for **Camp David of the Ozarks**, a place for children of the King of Kings!

What's going on with Camp David of the Ozarks?

Not much has been going on with CDO in December, because of the holidays. The biggest thing was we mailed out **260 newsletters**, which is more than double the number of people that have been on our mailing list in the past!

This month we will have our second board meeting, and set some dates on the calendar. We will also begin contacting other pastors and asking them to be a part of the ministry of Camp David. We need this to be a community effort to reach the children of prisoners in Southeast Missouri. We need prayer support, financial support, work teams, and caring people who will sponsor a child to go to camp.

The highlight this month will be the CCI / USA Ozark Sectional—a three day get-away for Ben and me, where we are challenged and encouraged through the seminars and talking with other camp directors. The dates for this are January 27-29. Please pray for our kids and Aunt Elizabeth while we are gone!

You are invited to a Clearing Party! On January 17th and February 28th we are having some clearing parties to clear land for power lines, the covered wagons and the dining hall. If you and/or your family would like to join us as we work, laugh, and get dirty, please let us know and we will be sure to make enough lunch for everyone!

Praises - Let's praise the Lord together!!

Praise the Lord for several gifts this month totaling $320. We have also received a lot of encouragement and prayer commitments from caring individuals.

Prayer Requests - "Casting all your cares upon Him..."

- Pray that we would be able to share the ministry of Camp David with other churches, and that they would join with us in reaching children of prisoners.
- Pray for people – families, adults, and youth, who can volunteer time to help **CLEAR LAND**!
- Pray for the finances to build **covered wagons** (our cabins). They cost less than $1300 each to build. We also need to: build a **pavilion/ dining room** with a kitchen and bathrooms; have a **well** dug before spring; and run **electric** to the back part of the property where we are going to build the pavilion.
- Pray for **counselors** and a **camp nurse** for camp in July.
- Pray for the children of prisoners - that they would be reached with the Good News of the gospel.
- Pray for our family as we try to balance our time between family, church, ministry, and work.

After reading this newsletter, I found another one with an exciting update on January 31, 2004:

"We just returned from our trip to the Christian Camping Conference in Arkansas, and have so much we want to share. It was a wonderful time of networking with other camps and learning valuable information... **God blessed us as the Ozark section cabinet voted to give a gift to Camp David totaling $1,420.00 which is more than enough to make our first covered wagon!**"

The funds for our first covered wagon were provided for. But that was just one of the things on our mile-long list, and we still needed to **build** the covered wagon cabin!

God provided funds for our first cabin— a covered wagon!

Chapter 8

Beer Parties and Ticks

We had a lot of obstacles to overcome to be able to start camp in just a few months. But our obstacles were nothing in comparison to the obstacles that our campers face. In light of the fact that is common for jailers to have grandpas, dads, and teenage sons from the SAME family all locked up, our campers were going to have to overcome a lot in order to break that cycle of crime in their lives.

To help you have a better picture of some of the things our campers deal with, I would like to share a letter from one of our campers, Holly. She and her brother came to camp for three years. Holly not only came as a camper, she was also invited back for our special training week for senior campers, which means we saw potential in her to become a leader. But something happened after that summer, and she moved and we lost contact. I pray that the things she learned at camp will come back to her in her journey. Here is a little picture of her life from her own pen.

"Well, I think it started when we lived in a trailer. I was really young and I was in the partying life (her parents were always having beer parties at her home). My dad would always have his friends over and we would always try to have a good time. But what I know now is that when my dad would have fun my mom would be slaving over everything, like cleaning and cooking, my dad was a clean freak, probably still is. Well we didn't have a washer or dryer, so one night when my dad had his friends over my mom was through with it all and she told my dad that she was going to call my grandma. So my dad went and got the phone and smashed it. Then my mom grabbed my hand, but she was soo mad that she forgot my little brother. When my mom spun around with me, I dropped all the money that my drunk friends had given me. We had to go back. Then later when my mom was at work, my dad invited one of his girlfriends over. Well, they both were drunk and high, and they had me and my brother drink beer. Then when my mom was at work again my dad took us out and went to his friend's house and he gave them weed. Dad's girlfriend took us to the store to give us candy. I remember my grandma mentioned that he grew pot at her house and that she would always kill it.

My dad always told me not to cry, he made that a rule and if I cried, he would give me a reason to cry. He would always make my mom do things that she didn't want to do and he would beat her. Then when my dad went to prison we moved and my mom

had all these relationships. I think in a way she was like trying to find love. She told me that the only guy she fell in love with was dad. I don't get that. But then my dad came back and when he found out that my mom was pregnant with another one of his children, he said that it wasn't his and he started calling her inappropriate names. He stayed but even though they weren't married- I call it an affair, well any way he broke the 7th commandment (we teach the Ten Commandants at camp so that's why she included this in her letter to us). *That's where my little brother that I have never met came in. Then one day my dad got really mad for some reason I don't know, and he started shouting and breaking and throwing our really heavy old coffee table at us, and it hit us, and I was so upset. Then the landlord came up and called the cops, and I had to go downstairs, and we watched my dad drive away (in the cop car) with a glare in his eyes. Then in prison, he wrote me a letter saying it was ok to cry. That made me even madder. Now I have a new baby brother. I think Dad is starting to get mean with (his girlfriend), my soon to be step- mom. And I'm thinking that the cycle begins again."*
~Holly

That Ain't Right! And this is why we have camp. To give hope to a group of kids who live in our neighborhoods and are wondering, "Will I grow up to be just like my dad? or mom? Is anything ever going to change? Does anyone care?"

There are people in our community that do care. They joined with us that spring in 2004, cutting down trees and dragging them out of the woods to make room to build our covered wagon circle. Working in chigger and tick infested woods; they also cleared a spot for our main meetings. One brave lady, a recent acquaintance, came out to help clear the land for part of an afternoon. She told me later that she found 96 ticks on her when she got home! Another lady from our church, Kathy Collins, was excited about our dream and offered to provide meals for us for a week so we could work on the land. Not only did Kathy and her daughter Sarah have to carry heavy coolers up and down a big hill to camp each day (we still didn't have a driveway to camp), but after bringing in meals and warming them over a campfire, Kathy stayed and worked all day. She worked alongside me to clear the land and trim trees with hand-held snippers. After a few days of using the hand-held snippers, I asked Ben to teach me to use his chainsaw! He did, but he insisted that I learn how to sharpen the blades and check the oil too. I became a "chainsaw chick" that spring! After I cut down medium-size trees that Ben had marked, Kathy would use the snippers to clean up the logs. The logs were saved for future building projects. Then all those branches we were cutting off were thrown onto large piles to burn. I discovered that cedar branches burn hot and fast, and I know I singed some eyelashes that week! After several days of working together, Kathy and I had scratches from the cedar trees all up and down our arms and big bruises on our legs. (All the other spots on our bodies seemed to have tick or chigger bites on them!) We learned that the sap from cedar trees can only come out with cooking oil, so even cleaning our clothes was a challenge. We really felt like hard core missionaries (and a little crazy too!). I was concerned the hardships would scare Kathy away, but she actually volunteered to be our camp cook that first summer! She even came back as our Food Service Director for four more years!!

During that week of clearing the land, Ben and I set up a tent for our family next to the area we were clearing land in order to save time and energy walking up and down that hill. I felt like a real pioneer woman as I cooked over a campfire and heated water to give my kids baths that week. Our kids loved camping out and thought it was all a grand adventure!

It was a miracle happening before our eyes, with all the projects that God brought together. In two and a half months we took virgin land and: dug a well, ran electric, set up a pool, put in a rough driveway, fenced in a petting zoo, and built a cook shack, outhouse, shower house (it was camp style—no roof!), and two covered wagons. The last hurdle was where we would meet. We didn't have the time or money to make a pavilion like we had originally planned. Another camp heard of our need, and gave us a big old army tent which seemed like an answer to our prayers! But the tent was only set up for a day when a strong wind storm come through and tore that worn-out tent to pieces!

The shredded army green tent pieces lay all over the game field. And camp was to start in a week.

Building the 1st outhouse!

9 x 11 foot Kitchen Shack

Our family in 2004

The shower house

God brought so much together in 2 1/2 months!

Chapter 9

I Have a Father

Why is it that, so often, when things don't go as we think they should, we think our Heavenly Father doesn't really care? Did our Heavenly Father care that the army tent that was donated was ripped in shreds all over our field? Did He care that we had worn ourselves out trying to clear the land, only to come to a stand-still?

We sang a song during our first year of camp that has become a favorite. We sing it each year and the campers never tire of it. We all need to be reminded of these truths...

"He Knows My Name"

by: Tommy Walker

"I have a maker

He formed my heart

Before even time began

My life was in his hands.

He knows my name

He knows my every thought

He sees each tear that falls

And He hears me when I call.

I have a Father

He calls me His own

He'll never leave me

No matter where I go"

While some of our campers have a mom in prison, most of them are fatherless. When they come to camp and learn that God wants to be our Father, it grabs their attention. Their hearts are aching from the pain of rejection and abandonment, and this song tells them there is a God who sees their tears and wants to be their Father.

Cliff and Susie Johnson encouraged us to pick "camp names." They were known to their campers as "Chief Big Tick" and "Mother Hen." I chose the name *Lady Rose*, because I love roses and I love to make things beautiful. (Superpower fact: If I had a super power it would be to transform something that looked like junk into something of value and beauty!) Over the years, I have changed my title to *Mama Rose*, reflecting how God has given me a *mamas'* heart for these kids. Ben coined the phrase, "Big Heart," and added "Sheriff" as the title, but he would change the title each summer with the theme we were doing. He has been, "Sir Big Heart," "Commodore Big Heart," "Coach Big Heart," etc. The title the campers and I like best is "Papa Big Heart." Ben chose that title during our 2010 African theme, and it has stuck. I think the kids like knowing they have a papa at camp. One boy even told everyone that Papa Big Heart was really like a dad to him.

Our real desire was to point these kids to a loving Heavenly Father. Hope was one little girl who learned about her Father God during our early years of camp.

Hope and her two sisters came to camp from a rough neighborhood in St. Louis. Her sister said their mom was very busy with her work and boyfriends, and at times there was not enough food in the house for the girls. Hope got sick off and on during camp, but whenever she spent one-on-one time with our camp grandma, "Grandma Denise," she felt better. At the special Princess Dinner the last

Princess Hope found true hope in Christ.

night of camp, Papa Big Heart talked to the girls about how

most of them have daddies in prison and about how they miss them. Then he explained that God says he will be their Daddy, and the girls can talk to their Daddy God at any time. This message touched a raw nerve in Hope, and she sobbed as she told Grandma Denise that she doesn't have a daddy to talk to. Denise held her and explained how she could know God as her Daddy and that He would always be there for her. That night Hope decided to trust in God as her Daddy. The next morning she left camp with a smile on her face and hope in her heart.

Our Daddy God took care of us too. Within a day or two of losing our meeting tent, a friend of Ben's parents, Loraine Mathis, contacted us and offered to let us use her red

This revival tent served as our meeting place for three summers!

and white revival tent for our two weeks of camp! Loraine ended up loaning us that tent for three summers!! God is so good and faithful.

We got the names of the kids to invite to camp from Angel Tree, a branch of Chuck Colson's Prison Fellowship. That first summer, 18 kids came over two weeks of camp. Four young ladies from our local community were daring enough to be counselors, and two young men came—one even flew out from Pennsylvania to be a counselor! There were a total of 20 volunteers that made Camp David a reality. One of Ben's customers that he had done remodeling for, Maria Carroll, offered to take the role as "Camp Nurse" to oversee the health side of camp. Maria was our nurse for nine years!!

We had goats and bunnies in the petting zoo and one horse that I led around and gave the campers horse rides on. Ben taught the Bible lessons with flannel graph, and we had our first birthday party under the big tent. Ben's parents opened their home and hosted our first Princess dinner in their basement. By the end of those two weeks of camp, we were exhausted. Not only had we worked like crazy to get everything built and ready for camp, but during camp our family had pitched a tent in a little grove of trees near the revival tent, and camped out with our three little ones. By the end of those two weeks, I was so ready to get back to my soft bed, and our own bedroom.

In spite of all the challenges (and ticks!), I was hooked on this dream of giving hope to children of prisoners.

Chapter 10

Donuts Anyone?

Fundraising. Ben and I will admit it isn't our favorite part of the camp ministry. But, when God called us to start a camp, we knew it wasn't ALL going to be fun. Ben would much rather break up a fight among campers than try to go out and raise funds. But then, we would have missed so many lessons God wanted to teach us if we didn't have to do fundraising! People often ask how we get our funding, assuming we are supported by a large church denomination or have government funding since we are working with at-risk kids from St. Louis. Neither are true. We are supported by several local churches from different denominations and by the body of Christ across America. We also give effort to some fundraisers. Some work better than others...

Do you know how many donuts are in 1,600 dozen boxes? 19,200 donuts. That's how many we purchased hot and fresh from the Krispy Kreme donut store in St. Louis very early in the morning on April 17, 2004.

With our first camp only a few months away, we needed a big fundraiser. One that would raise a lot of money. When we prepared for our mission trip to Guatemala, we did a car wash together as a fundraiser, but we only raised about $180 which was not going to be near enough money. I had heard of another group in the Rolla area that annually did a Krispy Kreme Donut fundraiser. They would sell 2,000 dozen donuts and raise about $5,000. I was able to talk to a lady that had helped with that fundraiser and she told me several tips to make it successful. I was sure that we could do the same.

Thankfully we had some daring friends that were willing to help. Enough friends, in fact, to have seven teams of people staged all over the great city of Rolla (population 17,000). We had our first Camp David t-shirts printed by a friend that was starting a shirt printing business. We also printed a paper to hand out with each dozen sold that told the community what the fundraiser was for and how to reach us. It was also our first big chance to use our new logo that a friend had made for the camp, and have that logo handed out all over Rolla!

It was still dark when everyone met very early at the parking lot of the local grocery store. We gave each of the seven teams over 100 dozen boxes, and Ben put hundreds of extra donut boxes in our vehicle. His plan was to drive in a route to each of the selling spots and check on how everyone was selling (and hopefully restock!). Before heading out, everyone gathered into a circle for prayer. God had already answered one prayer in that it wasn't raining that morning!!

The selling began. The corner of Kingshighway and Hwy 63, was the busiest. Ben kept in steady contact with each team. We started getting reports back that were all sounding the same. While sales were going okay, there was a common answer when drivers were asked if they wanted fresh donuts. "Sorry, I've started a diet!" Then it hit us. The Atkins diet had just become very popular— a lot of people we knew were on it. But it had never occurred to us that it might affect donut sales! By noon it was really hot and no one wanted donuts. We announced it was quit time and gathered all the extra donut boxes together. We had sold 1,200 boxes of donuts, but there were still 400 leftover boxes (that's 4,800 donuts). We only raised about $1,700 from the donut fundraiser, and we knew we couldn't freeze the 400 leftover dozens to serve at camp. So we took them around, early Sunday morning, to local churches and gave them away. Later I learned that the other group that had usually sold 2,000 dozen donuts in Rolla had also had a significant drop in sales that spring. I guess we had caught the end of what HAD been a good fundraiser. But the amazing thing is that, even though our fundraiser raised fewer funds than we had hoped, God still provided for us to have our first camp in July through many individual donors all across America.

The next year, we began to talk about constructing a multi-purpose building in place of the big, hot tent. During camp, the borrowed tent would sit on the spot that we hoped to build on. Of course, constructing a **big** multi-purpose building would require a **big** fundraising plan. At our camping conference, I learned a little about grant writing and even sent one proposal out, but it was rejected by the foundation because of our location. Several board members began encouraging us to apply for Missouri Tax Credits. *Called, Anointed, Sent* was the ministry that loaned us the revival tent, and they had applied for MO tax credits and were awarded 70 percent credits. The tax credits enabled donors to give large donations which actually only cost a little out of pocket for them. For instance, if a blessed donor wanted to give $1,000, the ministry would get that full amount, but after all the tax credits were applied, it would have been less than $100 actually out of their pocket.

Called, Anointed, Sent let us look at their paperwork that a non-profit had worked up for them to apply for the tax credits. As I pored over the paperwork, I felt we could fill out the application without having to go through another non-profit to do it. So I got to work. Sitting for hours at my little desk in our camp office (also our kitchen!), God gave me wording to answer the questions. One of the points on the application was easy to respond to: *One outcome addressed by CDO (Camp David of the Ozarks) is: "Decrease the number of crimes against persons or property." Without positive role models, children of prisoners and other at-risk youth will likely walk in the footsteps of their parents. A week of camp with one-on-one mentoring gives these children positive role models. CDO's camp program includes lessons on good morals and the destructiveness of drugs and alcohol abuse. The campers are encouraged to not participate in crime, or gangs, but to become involved in church, community, and other civic activities.*

Although I had understood it would be a long, time - consuming process of applying for the tax credits, it wasn't until I had almost finished with the application that we learned that the earliest we could hope to have our application be accepted would be the following summer and that it was likely to take several years. It was discouraging enough to just give up on that method of raising funds, but we pressed on and submitted our application in early November.

On December 20, 2005, we were shocked and thrilled to hear that CDO had been granted $179,400 in Missouri NAP income tax credits, by the Missouri Department of Economics. We really believed this would allow the camp to raise the estimated $358,800 for the multi-purpose building we wanted to build. We even dreamed of breaking ground on the new building in March.

While this was an incredible answer to prayer, we were disappointed to learn that we were only awarded 50 percent credits since the camp had a Rolla address. If we had lived just one more mile out of town to the west, we could have gotten 70 percent credits, which we quickly learned are MUCH easier to "sell."

So despite our inexperience with fundraising, Ben now began the adventure of meeting people in the corporate world and inviting them to be part of the Camp David dream. While Ben hoped to spend the next three months "selling" tax credits and then begin overseeing the building project, the reality was that he still had to provide for his family. So he would spend a few days remodeling homes, then he'd change his painter overalls for a dress shirt and slacks and visit businesses. After several months, Ben had been able to "sell" about $7,000 worth of tax credits, which was a great start, but not anywhere near the amount we needed for the new building! Most businessmen in the area told Ben they would give a lot more if we had 70 percent credits.

What could we do with $7,000? Put a foundation in! And God provided for that in a huge way. A Mennonite youth group from Lancaster, Pennsylvania asked if they could come in August, 2006 for a week-long mission trip. The Bowmansville Mennonite group brought 40 strong workers as well as $2,000 from fundraisers to contribute toward the project. Then Bloomsdale Excavating, a local company, offered to do the excavation for the new building as a donation, and we were on our way to having a foundation!

While all this work of fundraising was occuring, I had been busy as a mom too. Not only was I homeschooling my oldest two girls; I also gave birth to baby number four. It was my hardest pregnancy, and ended with a very difficult birth in which we had to transition from a home birth to a hospital birth, and I still hemorrhaged. We named our little girl Katherine Hope. The "Hope" was what God was teaching us during that part of our journey. The summer of 2006 found me pushing a baby stroller all over camp and the campers were always asking if they could hold my baby! Even the little boys would run over and sit beside me and ask to hold my baby. After about 10 seconds they would hand Katy back to me, and then run back to their team. But I loved sharing my baby with them!

That August, as I walked around the forms for the concrete pour on the foundation and stepped over the steel rods laying in what would become the floor to our building, I cried. I thought of all those really hot days in that revival tent, and the scares we had when big storms came through and it looked like the revival tent would blow away (and my baby was in the stroller in there!). Then I thought of our ground breaking day a few weeks prior and all the friends and pastors from the community that had come out to celebrate with us as we put our shovels in the soil and turned it over. Then I thought ahead to the next step...

We didn't know how to get to the next step. We knew we couldn't sell any more tax credits in our area, which after all the time and effort I put into filling out that application, that was a big let-down. But the foundation was being laid so we couldn't turn back. We had to trust God to take us from having a foundation, to building on top of it.

God sent the Bowmansville Mennonite Church group from 950 miles away to help get the foundation set.

Chapter 11

More Than Enough

We met Chris at our local county fair. We had a table set up at the fair for Camp David, and she was across from us with her Pampered Chef table. Our four children attended the fair with us, although my baby Katy was eight months old at the time, so she stayed in the stroller. We noticed that Chris had a lot of kids hanging around at her table too, and we got to talking. You never know when you begin talking to someone what is going to happen down the road.

Chris introduced us to her 18-year-old daughter Amy who volunteered to help me in the office! A big project Amy took over was doing graphic design and creating the newsletters that we sent to the campers each month. That fall Amy met my brother Andy at a camp event, and a year later became my sister-in-law! Amy's sister Debra served as a counselor at camp the next summer and met her husband-to-be who was also on staff! Over the years, Chris' family has been a huge blessing to camp as five of her daughters have served on staff (and continue to serve!) One daughter, Laura, even served as an intern at camp for seven months and was a great help with graphic design.

Something happened that first year after meeting Chris that was a complete miracle from God. Chris had reserved a booth for her Pampered Chef products at a large BMW bikers event and learned that each year the bikers raised money for a non-profit organization in that area that helps kids. Chris boldly suggested that the organization choose Camp David for their project that year. A few weeks later we received a phone call that shocked our socks off! The BMW bikers group wanted more information about the camp because they were considering us!!! That initial phone call was followed by several others. By early spring of 2007, we knew we had been chosen!!

The bikers group didn't promise how much would be raised, but they did say that the year before it was around $20,000!! That would be enough money to get a good start on our multi-purpose building!! When we had tried everything we could do to raise the money for the new building, God chose to provide for the start of it through a group of motorcyclists.

Because the revival tent was not going to be available for summer camp 2007, CDO's board of directors voted to take out a loan to begin purchasing the building materials so we could get the front part of the building framed in before summer camp. The hope was that when the BMW bikers event happened in late August we would have the $20,000 to pay back the loan. Many volunteers came out that May to get the new building framed. We barely got the roof on and the concrete floor swept before camp started, but God brought it all together. It was just the shell of a building—no insulation, drywall, plumbing, etc. But it was a whole lot better than the tent!

This is fort Turley, just two weeks before camp started!

As camp ended, Ben became concerned thinking of the risk the camp had taken when they borrowed money for the building materials on the hope that the bikers group would come through. Then it was the end of August, and the anticipated event had arrived. Here is Ben's account of that night in 2007...

"Surrounded by a group of 400+ bikers, I was excited and tense. Excited because this gift from the BMW Curve Cowboy Reunion would likely be the largest gift Camp David (CDO) had ever received. Tense because of all the doubts and questions like,

"Would it be enough or had the board acted presumptuously when it decided to take out a loan in lieu of this event?" I kept quieting my fears with the truth that CDO is God's camp, and He loves these children even more than I do.

To my excitement and relief the evening was filled with one generous donation after another including a new video projector! There were gifts from vendors, instructors, raffle winners, and finally the fundraiser check for $22,000. This was enough to pay off the building loan and finish some other camp projects like the kitchen porch!"

God is so faithful. The $20,000 bank loan in 2007 was the only bank loan Camp David has ever had. After that bikers event, the board of directors voted to set a policy that camp will never again borrow money. So construction has at times been slow, and things have taken a long time to finish, but we have kept to that policy and God has provided for our needs.

Many have asked why we named this new building, "Fort Turley." Just as with Chris, we don't know how the people we meet along the way may become significant in our journey. When Ben and I first moved to Missouri, Ben needed work. He began knocking on doors in Rolla, and Judge Turley was one of the first to hire Ben to fix up some things around his home. As the years passed and Ben continued to do good work for the Turleys when they needed it, Ben shared about our dream of starting a camp and they were very enthusiastic about the dream. At Judge Turley's passing in 2007, it was suggested that we name our new building in honor of him. Here is the announcement that was in our local newspaper:

"Camp David of the Ozarks is proud to announce that they will be naming their new multi-purpose building "Fort Turley" in honor of the late Judge Bill Turley who was a supporter of the camp. Turley was known for his fair justice by police, attorneys, fellow judges, and even the guilty. The Turleys began supporting the camp soon after it started. Before Mr. Turley recently passed away, he had asked that gifts be sent to his church and Camp David of the Ozarks instead of flowers. Katharine, the wife of the late Bill Turley says, "Bill would often say it was the children of prisoners that got the hardest sentence." Smith says, "When it was suggested to us that the building be named in honor of Judge Turley, I liked the idea. I thought it would be neat for the campers to be inspired by stories of his life and his legacy of humble, honest care for his fellow man."

Sometimes it is easier to trust God to provide for the ministry, than for our own family. During those years, we lived in our remodeled home next to Ben's parents' home during the school year and then move into an RV during summer camp. After several summers of living in RVs during camp, I really struggled with the thought of doing it again the next year. I wanted to move to the camp—not right in the middle, but on the edge so it would be just a short walk to Ft. Turley. I wanted my kids to be able to sleep in their own beds, not in sleeping bags on the floor, for the entire summer. I also wanted to be able to do some of my laundry during the week for our family of six, and we really needed an office at camp. Could God provide more than enough for our family to live in a home on the camp property year-round?

One of my favorite hymns is *His Eye is On the Sparrow.* The song ends with this: *"His eye is on the sparrow, and I know He watches me."* He was watching out for us. In an unprecedented way, our family received several large personal gifts that fall that we were able to save towards a down-payment on a house. I began to dream of a home, and despite my dislike for mobile homes, it seemed like the cheapest way for us to go. I spent time each day looking at classifieds online—from our own, "Rollanet Classifieds," to the St. Louis Dispatch. It was an up and down adventure as several good possibilities fell through. The one we finally settled on was a bank repo: a 1998 model, 2100 sq. ft. double wide with 4 bedrooms, an office, two baths and my favorite feature—a fireplace. We signed a contract on it in late November, but weeks later we learned that the bank decided it was worth $10,000 more than we expected. The broker we were working with suggested we make an offer to the bank, and to our great surprise they accepted it! One of the sad things for me as I cleaned out that re-possessed home, was that throughout the house was a trail of socks, underwear, award ribbons, and photos from the family that had previously lived there. I wondered what kind of distress could have left this crazy mess. Then I saw on the kitchen counter beside the moldy bread, a clue. It was a little paper with a phone number scratched on it: the Domestic Violence Hotline. That poor mom must have left in a real hurry to protect herself and her children.

It was quite a job getting the house site ready with all the snow and rain we were having. At one point, the excavator said that we would

Our new home- at camp!

need to find a new site because the ground was too wet! But with God's blessing, lots of perseverance and the help of family and friends, the site was prepared and the mobile home was moved here on January 12, 2007. We got busy hanging trim, fixing waterlines, hooking things up and painting. One month later we moved in, and the "new" house felt like a dream home to us! We looked forward to entertaining guests and camp staff in our new home and anticipated summer camp being a lot less stressful with our residence and office being right here! (Years later, I would begin to rethink that last point, but you'll hear that story later!) Throughout the whole adventure with all the disappointments and fears, we kept hanging on to the truth that **God delights in giving good gifts to his children.** Looking back we can see His hand all along the way. **God is good. He is more than enough.**

We would remember these stories of God's provision years later, when it looked like we would have to shut down camp in the middle of a summer due to lack of funds.

Chapter 12

No Chain Link Fences

Ben once told a man, "*We run a summer camp for children of prisoners.*"

"*How do you control them?*" the man responded with a look of concern. Ben could almost see his mind running to **razor wire, chain link fences, and guard dogs.**

Quickly, Ben reworded what we do, "*the camp is for children who have a parent in prison.*"

"*Oh!*" he said, and his face brightened.

Our campers aren't criminals. In truth, they are victims. Victims like Tyrell and his brothers who were abandoned by their mother and now face life without mom OR dad since their father's incarceration. Victims like Marcus who hangs his head in shame and mumbles when asked about his father in prison. Victims like Maria and Josie, whose father was sentenced to 26 years for abusing them.

The problem is huge. Nationally, one in 33 minors has a parent in prison. Missouri alone has about 40,000 children of prisoners. As a result of their parents' incarceration, these young people make up two out of three juveniles in the correctional system. The correctional system is costing Americans over $70 billion a year.

Does going to camp and learning new ways to respond to life (with other kids just like them) change anything? Does helping prisoners' children learn positive ways to resolve conflicts make a difference? Does teaching them about God's love and sharing stories of how God turned people's tragedy into triumph give us hope for them? According to an in-depth study on at-risk youth, these camp experiences are key factors that will significantly alter the course of their lives.

Here is a portion of a letter we received from Laura L. Valenti, who is a former Jail Administrator. *"Although I worked 10 years with the Laclede County Sheriff's Department, the last three and a half of which, I ran their 100+ bed jail, I've never seen a program with more potential to break the cycle of crime that we so often see in families, as children of criminals become the new generation of prisoners, living out what they see each day. Camp David offers boys and girls a choice, a serious look at a different way of life, based in Christian love. Children who know too much about drugs, alcohol, violence and the life that they bring, get an opportunity to live in Christian community with adults who treat them with love, laughter, and respect. If you are truly interested in doing something to combat drugs, violence and crime, I can think of no more personal or effective way of doing that than opening your heart to Camp David of the Ozarks. This is one of those rare places that is truly fighting crime in our society, at the root cause."*

At Camp David, our counselors pour the love of Christ on these kids. Marcus lights up and grins from ear to ear when he talks about wrestling in the pool with his counselor. Lanell and his brothers can remember holding their counselor's hand as they walked to the dining hall. And, at camp, Maria and Josie feel safe to give and receive hugs. Camp is a place where the joys and sadness of these kids are noticed and shared.

One of the sad things that kids learn as they grow up in families involved with crime is that life is hard. If you want to survive, you have to fight. Here is a story from Ben about a fighter that came to camp…*"Monday afternoon I received the news that the St. Louis bus was heading to camp with 11 boys, instead of 15. One boy just didn't show, and another three (brothers) were lost somewhere en route with their aunt. Being a father, I could only imagine the three boys sadly driving back home in a hot car after hours of hopelessly trying to catch the* bus. I quickly began calling friends in St. Louis, trying to find a driver to bring the boys to camp, as I quietly prayed. I also reached the discouraged aunt of the three boys, and assured her not to worry—we would get them to camp. Talking to my wife, Grace, I learned that when she had called that morning, the aunt had forgotten about camp. She had only one hour to throw the boys' clothes together, and rush out the door to try to reach the St. Louis pick-up spot. Five hours later, three tired brothers arrived at camp with our two staff members who had made the special trip. They had three pieces of luggage and one pillow. As dusk set in I helped the boys get settled in their cabin teams, while the staff found pillows and sleeping bags from our storage room. Over the next couple of days it became clear that 11-year- old Lanell (the oldest), was a fighter. In action and conversation, his counselors found that all his activities revolved around fighting. Fighting was his answer to every problem. It had won him arguments, acceptance, confidence, and even helped him out of difficult situations. I was concerned because fighting could be what would land Lanell behind a chain link fence. As the week went on, Lanell discovered God's gentleness and love. He began to desire something new. He told his counselor he wanted to "turn his life around" and be baptized. To our joy, Lanell put his faith in Christ, and was baptized the last night of camp. His change was evident in what followed. Dripping wet, Lanell went around and hugged each camper telling him, "You're my brother now!" The fighter had learned to love.

❦

Another summer there were two boys on the same team that were fighting much of the time. Every time I turned around, Ben was sitting down talking to those two boys. Personally, I would have sent those boys home because I just didn't think they'd ever learn. But as Ben patiently kept working with them, helping them to understand the importance of owning their wrong and apologizing, he began to see a little change in the two boys. So he sent them out to their morning activity classes. During the nature class our photographer captured

what became one of my favorite pictures— those boys in the Discovery Garden eating radishes with their arms around each other's shoulders. It was priceless! As the boys entered the dining hall after their morning

enemies or friends?

activities, one boy exclaimed, "*Papa Big Heart, I did what you told me to do! When I got mad at Jaheim, I didn't punch him, I just pushed him!!*" Well, it was a step. It was a step away from the direction of chain link fences. And we thank God for each little step we see.

Chapter 13

Scars on his legs

One day as the little boys were running towards the game field, one of them told his counselor, "*I LOVE camp!*"

"*Why?*" asked the curious counselor.

"*Because I can run around outside and not get shot!*" the boy said as he ran off. The counselor's head was spinning. Was that kid saying what he thought he was? Yes, sadly, that little boy was not allowed outside at home because of the gangs and frequent shots being fired in his neighborhood. I personally can't imagine trying to raise little boys in the inner city where it is unsafe to play outside. Camp is more than just a fun time— it is a chance to run outdoors and be safe from bullets for one week.

I recently realized that I do not have any relatives who died from being shot, yet many of our campers have experienced that trauma. One girl talked about how her grandpa shot and murdered her dad, and how she had to go help her mama find her dad's dead body. It is easy at times to get frustrated with our campers when they just don't listen, but then we hear about the pain they are carrying inside, and we wonder how they even go through each day with so much pain and loss.

Each year, as I read the camper's prayer requests, it hits me that their main request is, "*That I'll be safe.*" When you grow up hearing gunshots and seeing loved ones shot and die, you grow up feeling the world is unsafe. Some kids came to camp already having been caught in the middle of such violence. Here is Ben's account of one such discovery...

"I can still remember sitting beside 12- year-old Rahiem. We had just gotten out of the pool and were eating a snack when another camper begged him to tell how he got the scars on his leg. I glanced over and saw a star- shaped scar that looked very much like... a scar from a bullet wound? My eyes shifted to his face. Avoiding the questions of the other camper, Rahiem formed his fingers into the shape of a gun and looked over at me. I understood. Later I learned that he had been caught in the middle of a gun fight and was hit twice by bullets in the cross fire."

Sadly, Rahiem was not the only camper that has come with scars on his legs from being caught in the line of gunfire. It's happened more than once—and these aren't kids from war-torn areas of Uganda. They are from St. Louis, Missouri. There have also been campers with fresh wounds or scars which we have had to report as abuse and neglect.

Some of the scars our campers come with are on their arms and legs, from self-harm, otherwise known as cutting. Some of these cutters are only 8 and 9 years old. One camper arrived during a hot week in June with a hoodie (sweatshirt) on, and told her counselor she didn't plan to take that hoodie off all week. But as that camper experienced love and grace at camp, a few days later the hoodie came off and her counselor saw scars from cutting. Most children start cutting when there is an incredible amount of pain in their hearts. As that camper's hoodie came off, her face changed. Her features softened and she looked me in the eye more as I talked to her. She even asked about coming to serve on staff the next year, and I sensed she was beginning to value herself more.

Rahiem, the boy who had the scars on his legs, came to camp again the next summer. Now it wasn't the scars on his legs that we noticed. It was the scars on his heart. Not only were BOTH his parents in prison, but his Aunt Re-Re, who was just one year older than him, had recently committed suicide.

Re-Re had been one of our campers. She had come to camp for two summers. I remember her as one of the louder, "I'm gonna do what I want to do!" type girls. I don't know what it was that had hardened her heart to God, but she never professed to make a decision for Christ at camp. I believe buried under her tough mask was a very hopeless young girl. The next spring we sent an invitation to Re-Re to come to camp again. Then a relative called, "*Can you please take Re-Re off your mailing list? She died and we'd like you to stop sending the newsletters and camp stuff.*" I asked a few more questions and realized it wasn't a car accident, the cause of death was suicide. I was stunned. With a shaking hand, I called a friend in St. Louis. Within a short time this friend had found the headline in the newspaper that simply read, "*13 year old girl hangs herself*" That girl had been one of our girls. One of our girls without hope.

In Loving Memory of Re-Re, one of our girls without hope.

The reality is that sometimes there is nothing we can do, and sometimes our best efforts to help the hurting fail. We can show love unconditionally, and tell the "Good News" that God so loved the world, and young people still make their own choices.

Rahiem made a choice on his way home from camp. It was just a little thing, but after a very emotional week with him, we were excited to see a little hope. The church van was heading down the highway and it was packed full of boys going home after a week of camp. Camp Counselor Joel was riding as chaperone to keep the campers in line. The boys were rowdy and loud, which is common when they are heading home. Then one boy said something mean about another boy's mama. The offended boy turned around and started hitting the other boy. Things went from bad to worse. In the middle of the fight that broke out, one skinny little kid threw his shirt off and lunged for the side door on the van. He was trying to escape while they were moving 70 miles an hour down the highway!

At the same time, Rahiem was in the back of the bus hurling water bottles to the front of the bus. As counselor Joel tried to restrain the wanna-be escaping camper, he called to Rahiem to help him. It was the first time all week the campers had heard Joel raise his voice and, while the words weren't mean, they were with authority. Rahiem responded by sitting up straight, and he stopped throwing water bottles. He then started telling the other boys to cut it out, and to settle down. Immediately things became calm. Rahiem was the oldest camper in the van, and the other boys listened to him. What happened next was a miracle. The campers, who four days earlier had only known how to solve conflict by fighting, were now apologizing to each other. They went on to talk about the Ten Commandments and all they had learned at camp. Joel later reported that while he never wanted to repeat another wild ride like that, he wouldn't have traded the sweet spirit in the van after the fight for anything.

Yes, these kids have a lot of scars, on their legs and hearts, but there is hope for them.

Another counselor, Sarah, shared this testimony about her senior girls and the hope Camp David held out to them.

"My campers came to Camp David deeply scarred, but with a miraculous tenderness for spiritual things. I appreciated the way Camp David reached them where they were, and inspired them in a way that was real, honest, and relational. One of my campers went from believing God hated her to feeling overwhelmed with His love, and committing her life to Christ. Girls worked through past issues and unresolved fear, anger, and grief. Camp David does an excellent job of first listening well, then pointing the girls to healing in Christ. To God be the glory!"

Chapter 14

Outhouse Smoking

Ben shares this story... *"Sending campers home is one of the most difficult jobs I have. This time was no different. I had checked and cross checked all the evidence, and the fact was that this camper, Ruby, had been secretly smoking in the outhouse. I guess the smell in the outhouse made it a good cover for the smoke smell, because none of the counselors caught it. It was another camper, a 15-year-old girl who had left her baby with her foster mom so she could come to camp, who told the nurse what was really going on. Ruby had also figured out a clever way to hold her cell phone under her shirt, and lean back in the back corner of her wagon cabin so she could talk to her boyfriend. Another very troubling situation I was dealing with was a report that the senior girl campers were sneaking out of their cabins at night, but no one would fess up to what they were doing when they sneaked out. When we confronted Ruby about the outhouse smoking, she denied it. I shared with her how addictions drive us to do things we hate and isolate us with the fear of others finding out. I encouraged her to be strong and ask for help, but she wouldn't talk. When Ruby's dad arrived (her mom is in prison), she was confronted with the stolen lighter and cigarettes that we had found in her backpack, but she still remained hard. Her Dad spoke to us of the troubles he had had with her, including stealing and said that she was headed right for the juvenile home. Before Ruby left we held hands and prayed for her. It was hard to see her go."*

Since Ruby was a local girl, I would run into her grandma from time to time in town. The following winter after sending Ruby home, I learned from her grandma that Ruby was doing better in school and seemed to be making some good choices. We were especially thrilled to get a long letter from Ruby talking about how she was reading her Bible and wanting to do good in school. But over the years, things went from bad to worse as Ruby's mom, while in prison, would make lots of promises for a better life. She would tell Ruby she loved her, and things were going to be different when she got out of prison. Then when she got out she'd go right back to her old druggie friends and in no time would be back in jail. I don't know the details of why, but Ruby ended up spending her 16th birthday in juvie camp. I prayed for her a lot during that time, and was so excited when her Grandma told me she was getting out! Once Ruby was back at her Grandma's house, I picked her up and took her out for supper. At that point she really wanted to make some changes and was planning to go to school to be a nurse. Then many months passed, and I learned that Ruby was living with a foster family in the area. I asked to meet with Ruby again hoping that, since she had wanted a fresh start, she might be interested in our new intern program when she aged out of the foster system later that year. I really didn't want her to be out living on the streets. Sadly, in the months since getting out of the juvie camp, it seemed that Ruby had lost all her focus on a fresh start. All Ruby could focus on that night was that her mom's new boyfriend was going to buy her a car when her mom got out of prison. My heart was so heavy as I left the restaurant. The cycle of broken promises, feelings of worthlessness, and crime was keeping her in bondage. Sometimes I still see Ruby driving fast through town...and I pray.

It shouldn't have been a surprise to us that some of our campers already have probation officers when they came to camp, but it was. Ben shares the story below about a boy that came to one of our early camps, who first had to get permission from his probation officer to come...

"It was our first day of camp in 2007. The campers had arrived a couple of hours previously, and were moving into their wagon cabins and finishing all the check-in procedures. All, that is, but John. At 14 years old, with sandy blond hair that hung over his eyes, he sat slouched in the front seat of his social worker's car. His arms were crossed and he was determined not to stay. After a bit of talking we finally convinced him to look around camp while his social worker was filling out papers (she left before he

got back to her car). John was still convinced that he wasn't
staying and when he saw the social worker leave, he took off
walking. Thankfully camp is surrounded by woods, and many
miles from town. I asked a staff member, Mark, to shadow him.
A short time later I met up with John and Mark down in the
woods talking. John was still resolved to not join his team and
wanted to sleep in the woods. As we talked about his options, I
learned that he had a probation officer for truancy, and he
hated participating in activities at school. After talking for an
hour, John guardedly joined his team. The next day we had the
senior boys work on a service project where they could learn
some construction skills. They were nailing some rough sawn
siding on the kitchen shack and I noticed that John was
diligently pounding away, hammer in hand, with a counselor at
his side encouraging him. As the week progressed John
commented to his counselor, "Here at camp, I am doing things I
always hated like reading and working, and I actually enjoy it!"
He also said that at camp he learned that God had a purpose for
his life. John never came back, but we pray that the seeds that
were planted will bear fruit. His life does have purpose."

Aaron was another boy that came to camp with permission
from his probation officer, although we didn't know it at the
time. Our office help, Becky, was making phone calls on
Monday morning reminding all the campers to be at their
pick-up spots, but when she called Aaron's home he said he
didn't want to go to camp. Becky told Camp Director Ben,

what Aaron had said, and he grabbed the phone and called Aaron's home. He talked with Aaron about five minutes, telling him all the great things he'd get to do at camp. But knowing teens hate to be controlled, he ended the conversation by simply saying that the bus would be at his pick-up spot at 1:00 pm. If he wanted a ride, he could be there, but if he didn't show up the bus would move on.

It was obvious who Aaron was when we saw him get off the bus. Tall, with a head full of blond hair, he had a scowl on his face that said, "*I hate everyone and everything.*" As much as possible, he stood at least ten feet apart from everyone else the rest of the afternoon. But the next day he was only about five feet from everyone else, and Tuesday night, after chapel, Aaron made a decision to follow Jesus. From that point on, things were different. Everyone on staff was remarking on the change they saw. Aaron became one of the most enthusiastic campers during song

Aaron was so excited to be baptized he let out a whoop when he came out of the water!

times. On Thursday, he decided he wanted to be baptized. We always call the camper's guardian to request permission before we baptize, and thankfully permission was granted for Aaron.

It wasn't until two weeks after camp that we got a call from the probation officer. She was so impressed in the change in Aaron since camp that she wanted to know how more of "her boys" could come to camp!! Ben called to check up on Aaron weeks later, and he was still really trying to make good choices and grow as a follower of Jesus.

Sometimes we are instruments in God's hands to make a difference, and that difference is easy to see. Sometimes we are just planting seeds and we never get to see the fruit. The challenge is to **keep pressing on**, doing what God has called us to do, whether or not we see the fruit of our love and prayers.

Chapter 15

Why Are They Important?

"Jesus put a child in the middle of the room. Then, cradling the little one in his arms, he said, "Whoever embraces one of these children as I do embraces me, and far more than me—God who sent me." Mark 9:36-37

When Ben and I got married, we were focused on how important Bible translation was. Many of the missionary stories we had read were about missionaries who translated the Bible into tribal languages. That seemed like such life-changing work. But God had clearly called us to children's ministry and not Bible Translation. In 2009 Ben's parents loaned him a book to read which really helped us to understand why having a ministry dedicated to reaching out to children was so important. Here is what Ben wrote after reading the book...

"Why are children so important to God? In a time when finances are tight, why should we be worried about reaching children of prisoners? Recently, I was given the book, Too Small to Ignore, by Dr. Wess Stafford of Compassion International. It

came at the perfect time as I was struggling with this question myself. Dr. Stafford pointed out that two-thirds of the people who give their lives to Christ do so before the age of 18. He also said that when we picture missions as masses of adults that are in need of Christ, we need to see that half of the mass would in reality be children. The Old Testament ended with a message about fathers turning their hearts to their children. Jesus placed such importance in children that he rebuked the disciples for not allowing the children to come to him in the middle of his teaching. He warned those who caused children to stumble of a fate worse than drowning. And he promised a reward for even the simplest act of giving a child a drink of water. Our childhood experiences shape our futures. The Bible heroes: Daniel, David, Joseph, and many more, found God as children and youth. They were able to stand in terrible adversity, resisted great temptation, and fearlessly faced death. All because somebody had told them of God's love and care for them. Can you remember the people in your childhood who helped you?

*There is more to the picture than children being needy. We **need** children. When Jesus' disciples were arguing about who would be the greatest in the Kingdom of Heaven, Jesus brought a child into their midst, and told them that unless they became like a child they would never enter the Kingdom of Heaven. We need children to show us what it is like to be God's children. When broken and shattered children meet the Father* *to the fatherless, it's earth shaking and we grasp an understanding of God's love for us in a way we never dreamed possible. Camp is a place where these things are possible."*

Camp is making a difference in the lives of children. The following story about two sisters from the fall of 2008 provides a glimpse of what camp can mean to these kids.

Gwen and Ra'shonda's faces were beaming as they arrived at our Banquet for Hope. As soon as Gwen saw her counselor from that summer, she ran to give her a hug and started to cry. Gwen's sister, Ra'shonda, ran over to Ben and I and gave us big hugs, with her brown eyes sparkling. This was our first benefit dinner in St. Louis and we had asked Ra'shonda to give a testimony at the banquet about what camp meant to her. Ra'shonda has been a camper for the past four years and the change in her life is nothing short of a

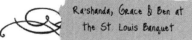
Ra'shanda, Grace & Ben at
the St. Louis Banquet

miracle. When we first met her, she was shy, and had a victim mentality that was constantly getting her into fights and arguments with other campers. That night she confidently shared with our banquet guests how much camp meant to her, how she had learned about God and how to respect herself. Sitting at our table, Ra'shanda's grandmother told us how Ra'shanda had taken her four camp photo albums (each camper gets a personalized photo album from their week of camp) with her to school and shared about Camp David with her class. For special music, Gwen and our daughter Bethany, sang our favorite camp song... *"I have a Father...He'll never leave me... He hears me when I call...And He sees each tear that falls."* As we looked at Gwen and Ra'shonda we could see that they knew their Father God cared for them.

One of the greatest joys in life is seeing a child that was beaten down with shame, sadness, fear and anger, encounter the love of God and be transformed into a beaming, confident, loving child.

This past summer Ben and I received a letter from a senior girl camper who has come to camp several times. Jenna is a beautiful, athletic girl who is doing great in school. Her mom is really involved with her life, and I'm sure is proud of her. But the day before Jenna came to camp she had gotten a letter from her dad in prison. In the letter her dad told her he no longer loved her, and he didn't want anything to do with her. That letter loudly spoke to that young lady that her daddy had rejected her and she was unlovable. She shared this with her counselor through tears during morning devotions. Two days later Jenna wrote us this letter. It is a heartfelt reminder of how important it is that we go out of our way to love and invest in the lives of hurting kids.

"I wanted to thank you guys personally. This camp means so much to me. I thought I was the only one who had a parent in prison, I always felt alone, abandoned, and worthless. When I found out about this camp, I was so thankful; knowing I am not alone means so much. I have made so many friends that I will never forget. This is not a normal camp. This camp is probably the best, special and most impacted camp I've ever been to. Just the fact I'm not alone is the best feeling ever. You two (Ben and I) have made a camp that is different from any other. Words can't explain how glad I am. Every year is so different, but has meant so much to me as any other year. Just, thank you for the great food, support, fun and people. Some of the best people I've met are from this camp. Thank you so much. I love you both so much and your family. Thank you for making camp so wonderful!" ~ Jenna

Chapter 16

Bestowing Value

We do a lot of unique things at this little camp with a big heart. We don't have a high ropes course, a lake, a gym, or long hiking trails—yet. But the unique things we do here have been carefully planned to make the most impact during a week of camp. Many of these things were learned from other camps that are working with foster kids, and troubled youth. While we can't take all the credit for them, we have seen their impact first hand.

One unique feature is awarding character certificates on the last night of camp. All kids need to be affirmed, but imagine the impact this has on kids that have a 7 out of 10 chance of going to prison. Campers have shared how they have been told over and over again that they are going to fail, they are worthless, and they are going to end up in the jailhouse just like their parents. Changing this cycle of crime and the futures of these kids starts with painting a new picture for them.

Every Thursday night when I go down to the campfire circle, I hold my breath in anticipation. This is my favorite part of the week. There is a lot of laughter, clapping, and even tears (especially on girls' weeks). After we sing some praise songs with the guitar, we listen as the counselors take turns handing out certificates that honor character qualities they see in each camper. They also tell stories of how each camper demonstrated those qualities that week. Sometimes it's easy to guess which camper they are talking about (like the camper who was always smiling!), but other times I can't figure out which camper it is. Then they call up one of the most difficult campers that week and I see an amazing example of God's love and grace. Despite how difficult that camper was, and how they may have cussed out their counselor or been ugly toward others on their team, the counselors have asked God for His eyes for that child. They chose to bestow value on them and see the good in each life. One tough young man was so pleased to receive a character certificate that he told Papa Big Heart he was going to frame it when he got home! Sometimes the campers have tears in their eyes while their counselors are talking about the good they saw in them, and I have a lump in my throat too.

Here is an early story from the campfire award's time, written by Ben:

"The sun was just setting. The staff and campers were settling around a small fire in the woods, on scattered lawn chairs and a circle of benches made from cedar posts and old cabin logs.

Outside the perimeter were three covered wagons, an outhouse, and a picnic table. Campers were putting sticks in the fire, and making boy comments. Slouching across from me sat Pyro (his camp name), with his arms crossed and a sad/angry look. He was 14 years old and a little overweight. His face was slightly flushed, with freckles, and he had a cast on his right leg. Normally he had a great disposition, but tonight Pyro sat there fuming about a spat with another camper at supper. Despite my best efforts, and the offending camper's apologies, Pyro was stuck, refusing to forgive or enjoy anything at camp.

I stood and asked the last of the boys to sit down, and introduced the next event which was Character Awards. Two college age team leaders in slightly-stained yellow camp shirts stood up. They pulled out some awards and one began, "This award is for Orderliness and Determination. This camper always knew where his things were and even set the stuffed animals in order ..." Pyro stood up with a slight grin on his face and puffed out his chest. They continued "...He also demonstrated determination ... by never complaining about his leg but just giving it all he had... This award goes to Pyro!" As everyone clapped, Pyro half-marched, half-limped over for his award. Later, after all the activities were over, I saw Pyro on the way to his wagon. I put my hand on his shoulder. "Are you still angry?" I asked. "No, everything's fine now." He said with a smile. "I forgave him." As Pyro realized his own value, he was able to extend forgiveness to someone who had hurt him."

Sometimes we don't even need a certificate. Just speaking value into the campers can have amazing results. Words like, "*You're not a bully, you're a child of God!*" or "*You're not trash, you're God's princess!*" Here is a story from Ben about Solomon, a camper who needed a new identity.

"*On Wednesday, Solomon had reached his limit and wanted to go home. He was done with the rules. So I asked the Counselor Coach to call his mother. Meanwhile, I talked to Solomon about how his decision will affect his future. He finally mumbled, "If I stay, I will just get in trouble again." God had given me the answer! Solomon's problem was that he saw himself as a bad kid. "Solomon," I said, "Remember how I told you about wise King Solomon in the Bible? I can tell you're a wise young man too by the questions you ask. The Bible tells us that even if a wise man falls seven times, he always gets back up. You made some mistakes. We all do. But you're a wise young man so you're going to get back up and beat this one. Let's go find the camper you hurt and apologize." Moments later Solomon had made it all right. Over and over during the rest of the week I would watch his face break into a confident smile. He even decided to follow Christ in baptism. His new identity gave him the courage to overcome.*"

Another way we bestow value is by having a birthday party each week of camp, and celebrating the campers' birthdays. Children from healthy, middle class, American families are used to big birthday parties with friends, cake, ice cream, and lots of presents. Children that come from homes caught in a cycle of crime, poverty, and neglect often don't know what it's like to be celebrated like that. Sometimes their birthdays are forgotten—maybe the adults in their life are high on drugs and the kids have to cook their own food if they want to eat. Maybe their mom wishes she could do something but there just isn't money or time to do anything because dad is in prison and she is working three jobs to try to provide.

In case you are wondering how celebrating birthdays makes a difference, I want to share this story from Ben...

"The first day and a half of camp, Kyle was complaining about not liking camp and dragging his feet. Everything he did was half-hearted. The second night, he had given up on camp so I let him call home to his mother. She explained to him in so many words that there was no way she was going to travel the two hours out to camp to pick him up, so he had better get his act together and follow the rules. He was compliant after that. Wednesday we learned that Kyle and another camper had a birthday that week. So we got two cupcakes, put candles in them, and sang, "Happy Birthday!" At first Kyle protested and said, "My birthday was Monday!" I told him it didn't matter, we wanted to celebrate his birthday because he was special to us. From then on his attitude steadily improved. Later that week he put his faith in Christ and even chose to follow him in baptism.

Sometimes it is the small gestures that say, "You're special!" that mean the most."

On Wednesday while the campers are out having free time, our staff begin to decorate Fort Turley with balloons and streamers. When the bell rings for supper, they line up behind Ft. Turley's doors, cheering and yelling *"Happy Birthday!"* as the campers come charging in. I remember watching one boy with a long scar on his face as he came into the building. He rarely smiled, but he couldn't stop the sparkle in his eyes or the smile that was pulling at his mouth as we were cheering that night!

There is always a lot of food at camp, and when the campers want seconds Papa Big Heart always asks a question. On the birthday night, he asks, *"What is the name of somebody special that was born on your birthday?"* It's funny to see puzzled expressions come over the new campers' faces as they try to think of someone famous that they've been told was born on the

What's the name of someone special, who was born on your birthday?

same day as them. The alumni campers jump up with sparkles in their eyes because they know the answer is "*ME!*" They run up to Papa Big Heart with their answers and he responds, "*Yes, you were born on your birthday, and YOU ARE SPECIAL!*" The new campers usually have this goofy grin as they walk away from Papa Big Heart, pondering the truth that while they may not be famous, they are special!

When they finish filling their tummies, our staff come out with birthday cakes and ice cream. Our cooks would have worked hard all day baking cakes and decorating them with each team's name on them. The cakes are set on each team's table and the candles lit. Then we all sing the "*Happy Birthday*" song, the candles are blown out, and a picture is taken to capture the special moment together.

The testimony below is from a young lady named Shawna, who served in the kitchen one week...

"One camper was so amazed by the whole birthday party experience. The staff had just served cake and I was coming around the tables to scoop ice cream. When he saw that he was getting cake AND ice cream, his whole face lit up with astonishment. He exclaimed to me incredulously, "This is ALL for US?" It broke my heart to see that he was delighted by such a small kindness and it made me think that maybe this was the first time someone had celebrated his birthday. At the same time though, I was so happy that I could make a difference. He

was so grateful and he hadn't even received his present yet. I answered his question with, "Of course it is! Because you're special and we love you guys!" It is for moments like this that I work at camp."

As the cake and ice cream are licked off the plates, we call the campers up by name to receive their birthday gift. Each birthday gift has a personalized card with it. The gifts are paid for by caring people in churches and other service organizations. We make this part of our *Fill a Backpack* program! Besides providing a flashlight, toothpaste, and shampoo for campers, those who fill backpacks also provide $10 towards the camper's birthday gift and a signed birthday card. We use the birthday funds to purchase special gifts such as a sports ball for the boys, or jewelry and sunglasses for the girls. I love watching the children's faces as they open their cards and read the encouraging messages inside them.

There is one more story I want to tell about the birthday parties. We were extra blessed for a few years to partner with the local UPS team to deliver the birthday gifts. Our office team would drop off the gifts and cards with the campers' names on them at the UPS center, and the employees there would volunteer their time to wrap the gifts in brown paper (like a real package that was mailed). Then at 6:30 pm, the UPS trucks would drive up in front of Ft. Turley, and honk their horn. Our staff knew they were coming, but of course, the campers didn't. Papa Big Heart would get the campers' attention, and say there was a UPS truck out front. Based on the excited yelling and running that happened at that moment, you would have thought a helicopter had landed in the big field! It was so much fun watching the kids crowd around that delivery truck, waiting to hear their names called so they could receive their special packages.

We are so grateful for each person that joins us in showing some of the most at-risk children in America that they are special and valuable.

I wish you could have heard the excited shouts when the local UPS team delivered the boys' birthday super soakers!

Chapter 17

I am beautiful!

My parents loved to dress me up in Polly Flinders dresses when I was a little girl. I played with dolls a lot (and made mud pies for them)! On special occasions my mom would put my hair in sponge rollers and I would have to sleep on those bumpy curlers all night. But it was well worth it because when my mom would take out the rollers in the morning, my hair would spring into ringlets, and my dad would affectionately call me, "Shirley Temple." I loved to get dressed up and spin around and around in my dresses. When I became a mom, I would sew dresses for my little girls. I loved to watch them spin around and around, giggling and squealing. What a shock to realize that many of the girls that come to our camp have never worn a dress. They've never had anyone sew them a dress or buy them a new dress for Easter Sunday. They've never spun around and felt pretty and feminine, or had their daddy look them in the eyes and say, "You're beautiful." But they get that chance to dress up and feel feminine at camp. We are probably the only camp that has an entire room full of jewelry, shoes, and formal gowns! From the horse-drawn carriage rides, to the served meal by our staff wearing white shirts, black slacks and paisley bow ties, to the white tablecloths, chair covers, and tall glasses, each part of the Princess Dinner says to the girls—"You are valuable. You are special."

formal dresses, elegant tables, and a served banquet say to each girl, "You are valuable!"

It is a lot of work to put on a "Princess Dinner" in the middle of a week of camp. It's not easy to find the "perfect" dress for 30 girls of various sizes and heights from our room of donated dresses. We use a lot of safety pins to make their favorite dresses fit! I recruit volunteers to come in and help do the campers' hair, nails, and make-up for two hours before the banquet. Once they are ready, a professional photographer takes formal pictures of each girl before the banquet begins.

From our Food Service Director to our Support Staff, everyone has to work extra hard that day. Many even give up their free time to get everything prepared! There is also a lot of extra clean-up afterwards. All those white tablecloths and chair covers that make it look so elegant have to be stain treated and washed!

Every bit of effort on our part is so worth it to see the change come over the girls. As the girls arrive back from their horse-drawn carriage rides and walk into the transformed Ft. Turley, their eyes are sparkling and they are giddy with excitement. While waiting for the other girls to finish their carriage rides, I watch these girls walk around and begin to spin...feeling that thrill for the first time of having your dress spin out around you, and feeling...beautiful.

Anna didn't feel beautiful when she arrived at camp. She was a spindly nine year old girl with a very short boy haircut, dark hair and brown eyes. With her parents constantly in and out of jail, Anna had lived with her elderly Great-Grandma from ages three to six. Then when she started first grade, she moved in with her Grandma, who was struggling with her health. As you can imagine, it's hard to experience a lot of "normal" childhood when your sole caregivers are elderly with failing health. When Anna got off the bus at camp, she fell in love with everything from the cabins to the bugs. She was over the top enthusiastic about everything. However, just before the Princess dinner, she drooped. With a note of resignation Anna sighed, "I am just not beautiful." Her counselor gently suggested that Anna close her eyes while she gave her a makeover. Anna sat doubtfully in the chair, her eyes squeezed tight, while the makeover commenced. When her counselor finished, she told Anna to open her eyes and look in the mirror. With astonishment in her voice, Anna declared, "Is that me? I'm beautiful!!" And she was.

Some of the girls don't want to put on dresses. At first, I reacted a little to their protests, but then someone that had more understanding in helping children shared with me that it is not uncommon for girls that have been sexually abused to feel "unsafe" wearing a dress. So we try to be understanding of their feelings and fears. I've even run to the store and purchased a few nice blouses, so the campers can keep their jeans on, but put on a pretty top and still get their special picture taken. Other girls wear their sport shorts under their dress, keep their cool sneakers on, and don't want make-up or jewelry. For these girls, it is important to extend grace and understanding of their reluctance. But sometimes gently nudging them to just try on a dress really is worth it.

One girl stands out to me on this. She had long, straight, ash blond hair, and wore it simply parted in the middle. Her wardrobe seemed to come from a boy's closet— baggy shirts and camouflage pants. She told her counselor numerous times she wasn't going to wear a dress at the Princess Dinner. Then Wednesday morning, all the other girls on her team were picking out their dresses and Julie was pulled into the Princess room. Her teammates were suggesting this dress and that, and she refused. But then a navy blue gown caught her eye. It was a simple design, nothing flashy about it, but it was a long gown, and Julie tried it on. It fit perfectly. Before she knew what had happened to her, Julie was standing in the dining hall in her navy gown with make-up on, her hair done up elegantly, and a few simple pieces of jewelry. We hardly recognized her. Not only was she dressed differently, she was standing different. She stood like a lady—with poise and grace. I believe that, inside her heart, all the things she had heard all week about how God had made her and had a special plan for her life were starting to come back to her. She was actually starting to believe she was valuable, and maybe even a little beautiful. Some walls came down that night, and we saw a new side of Julie. We saw her smiling and laughing, and she even danced with her counselor.

Sometimes that time of dancing for the girls and their counselors is the only time all week we see their walls come down. We are able for a short moment of time to connect with them. In all the excitement and fun music, they are able to forget the shame of having a parent in prison, and the pain of abuse, and become more childlike— laughing, spinning, singing. And then the moment is gone. Sometimes the walls go back up as soon as the pretty dresses and jewelry are taken off. Other times it appears that something was awakened in them and they are changed.

The change in another girl was very evident to everyone. Jessica and her sisters had come to camp for a few years. But this year when she got off the bus, she was different. She didn't look anyone in the eyes. Instead she mostly looked at the floor and her entire body language said, "I'm worthless." Knowing why her father was in prison, my heart ached and ached every time I saw Jessica. How could anyone hurt this precious girl? Her counselor said Jessica was in tears almost every hour, staring in the mirror and saying she was ugly. And every time she said she was ugly, her counselor gently spoke truth to her: "*You are beautiful.*" Jessica's counselor also spent a lot of time crying out to God for help, and for a breakthrough with this camper. She talked for hours with Jessica,

Shame is no longer her name—it is "Valuable."

sharing truths about how much God loves us and how He doesn't see us as dirty or ugly. Finally, at the Princess Dinner, as Jessica's counselor helped her get ready, Jessica paused in front of the mirror and said, *"I'm. . . beautiful!"* I walked by as Jessica was getting her formal picture taken, and I immediately knew something had changed. Jessica looked right at the photographer— and smiled. She was wearing a string of beads around her neck, and her counselor had done a special twist in her hair that was so elegant. Jessica was actually holding her head high instead of looking at the floor. The rest of the week, Jessica was a changed girl. She was more confident and happy, and if you were nearby, you could even hear her laugh a few times.

At my Grandpa Harkins' funeral last year I realized what a special gift he had given me as I was growing up. Grandpa would regularly tell me I was beautiful. Girls long to hear those words from a man in their life. If they don't hear it from their dads, grandpas, or brothers, they will look to other men for that affirmation. So during Camp David's Princess Dinners, that is the role my husband takes. Dressed in a suit, and taking the role of "Papa Big Heart," he goes around and greets each of the girls and tells them they are beautiful. And they blush, but their eyes sparkle.

Realizing that they are beautiful is so much more than focusing on outward appearance. When a girl sees herself as ugly and dirty, she feels she is worthless. And that makes her vulnerable to be a victim of sexual exploitation. She will give her body for easy sex, or sell herself for drugs to numb the pain. She also becomes an easy target for human trafficking. There is something we can each do about this. When we come in contact with little girls—whether we are Wal-Mart cashiers, or Sunday School teachers, we can seize every opportunity to speak words of life to them. We can be God's voice to say, "You are beautiful." I love this verse in Zephaniah 3:17, "*He will take great delight in you; in His love He will no longer rebuke you, but will rejoice over you with singing.*" Girls need to know that God delights in them, He sings over them. His love is more than we can ever imagine.

Recently I was thrilled as I listened to one of Ben's interviews with the campers. One girl, Christiana, shared what she had learned at camp—something I pray will protect her through her teen years. *"I learned that I am beautiful. That I shouldn't let anyone put me down because God is always there. And I was made by God, and God didn't make any mistakes in making me."*

Chapter 18

Talks with Papa Big Heart

Some campers stand out when they get off the bus. There
are those that are all smiles and are quick to come over and
give you a hug. There are those who walk with the
cool saunter and are quick to dominate the scene with their
loud obnoxious behavior. Ahmad was neither; camp was new
for him so he took the nervous "wait and see" approach.
Ahmad's sister and cousin had come the previous year
and thoroughly enjoyed it. Ahmad, his sister, and little brother
had been separated before their mom went to prison, and he
ended up over 1,000 miles away with his aunt and uncle (his
dad wasn't in his life at all, and his grandma was in prison
too). After six years of separation, Ahmad's mother got out
of prison, and the family was reunited a little before camp.
When the camp registration forms came out, his mother
signed them up for camp, but Ahmad wasn't sure what to
expect. His sister told him, *"Camp is neat. You learn about God
and stuff."* When Ahmad arrived, he was still unsure about the
whole idea. But by day two Ahmad had a whole different
outlook. He began eagerly learning about God, asking his

counselors questions about the Bible, and reading his Bible during his free time. He was even found lying in his sleeping bag late at night, reading his Bible with his flashlight in hand. This was the first Bible he had ever seen and it had awakened a desire to know God and His word. Ahmad also enjoyed talking to his guy counselors and Papa Big Heart, as there weren't any men in his life that he could talk to at home. Ahmad said, *"Camp was a place where I could open up and talk about things that I couldn't before."*

Every child needs a safe place to talk about their struggles. Through our years of serving children of prisoners we have identified six questions most of them struggle with:

- Is it wrong for me to love my father when he did so many bad things?
- Am I bad if I hate my father?
- People say I am just like my father, does that mean I will turn out like him?
- Is it my fault my parent is incarcerated?
- Did this happen because God hates me?
- What about the shame I feel?

In a small class, Papa Big Heart would ask the boy campers if they identified with these questions. At first they would look down in shame when they put up their hands up, but as the group time ended, their heads stayed up and they stayed connected with each other.

What did he tell them? Papa Big Heart told them that in loving their parent they were being like Christ, who loved us despite the things we had done wrong. He told them that when we are hurt, it is normal for us to respond in hatred or anger; he also shared that if we are going to heal we need to forgive and ask God to heal our pain. He talked about their fathers being created in God's image and that though flawed by sin, they still had some good qualities that were no doubt passed on to them. The boys can take the good qualities from their dads, and leave the bad. Last of all, Papa Big Heart told them true stories of great men who grew up in very difficult circumstances and how God used those circumstances to build greatness in them. As the boys left the class, you could almost **see** the weight of shame that had come off their shoulders, and the ray of hope that was in their eyes.

Sometimes I think one of the best gifts we give our campers is someone who will listen to their stories. Last summer two senior girl campers came to Ben and asked to talk with him. They said it was known around camp that Papa Big Heart was one that would listen to them. And they needed someone to listen to their stories. Someone to share their pain. Not someone to try to fix it, but to understand and care. Ben tells another story about a talk with two young men...

"The last evening of camp, 13 year old Mark's lips were tight with anger after an argument with another camper. John, the

other camper, had apologized for his part in the conflict but Mark wasn't talking. At this point I realized that telling him what the Bible said, or reasoning any more, would only further entrench him. I suggested we go out to the porch, where the two of us sat in rocking chairs around a checker board in the moonless night. Earlier that week he and I had talked about his family and how he got along with his mother. He told me about his stepdad threatening to kill his mother in front of the family. Later his stepdad left the home, but now he was worried about his stepdad's recent return and his mother's safety while he was at camp.

On the front porch, I built on our friendship by asking, "Mark, could you help me figure something out?"

Silence.

"The last night of camp some of the girls start to get moody and have bad attitudes. Their faces start to get hard and they stop talking. Do you know why that is?"

No answer.

I ventured some more, "Some of the boys have the same problem... Do you want to know what I think it is?" Mark nodded slightly, and I continued, "I think it has to do with the thoughts of everything they are going home to." Mark nodded in agreement.

"You know, it is really a sad thing." I sighed.

"What?" Mark responded.

I gently laid it out, "You and John... You could be friends. You
have a lot in common. You both have a dad in prison, you are
about the same age, and you are both guys."
After a pause Mark offered, "I didn't mean to say that to him, I
thought he was someone else."
Just then, like someone sent for him, out of the night walked
John onto the porch.
"I am sorry I said those things to you." Mark said.
"That's OK." John responded, with a smile.
Everything could have ended there but I pressed it a little
further, "Mark, why don't you tell John your story?"
Mark paused but then ventured out and shared about his
stepdad and the home situation.
Next John spoke up, "I know what you're feeling. I get in-
between my mom and her boyfriend when they fight. They tell
me to stay out—this is grown-up stuff, but I just want to keep
them from hurting each other. So I know what you're feeling. If
you want to talk about it, just tell me."
That night the two young men walked down to their cabins
with a new thought: "There is someone who understands what I
am going through. I am not alone in this."

They also knew that there were adults in this world, like Papa
Big Heart, who were unlike the adults in their homes. That
helped them to feel just a little more safe that an adult knew
their stories, and cared.

Chapter 19

Revealing the Father

My kids are proud of their dad, and feel safe with him. An incident at camp last summer reminded me of how different it is for kids who grow up with a dad in prison, who don't have a sense that Dad is a safe person.

Michelle, who was on our Leadership Team, was walking towards Ft. Turley one afternoon and overheard a conversation between a 15-year-old camper and my son, Timmy. This young man named Cortez was actually at camp that week because he had been invited back for a special training week for those older campers who showed potential to be on staff. Our goal is to develop leaders who will impact our world, and I think Cortez had started to take on some leadership because he was looking out for this kid he saw running around the hammocks next to the Ft. Turley. As Michelle walked by, Cortez was saying to my 10-year-old son, "You need to go find your counselor, now." Timmy replied, "I am fine out here." Cortez became more insistent. "No, you really need to go find your counselor **now**." But Timmy again just pushed it aside. (My kids live at camp year round, and it feels like home to them, which is why Timmy was pushing away Cortez's concern.)

Cortez got more urgent, and he looked at Michelle and said to my son, "What would you do if that lady came out here to do something to you?" Timmy answered, "I know her. She won't do anything to me."

Cortez could see he wasn't making any progress in trying to "protect" my son. He looked down the lane to camp, and then looked back at Timmy, trying to figure out how to convey his concern to my boy. He then asked, "What would you do if someone like my dad came down this driveway and was planning on taking you and hurting you? What would you do? You **need** to go find your counselor."

Michelle was impressed as she heard one of our campers taking the role of protecting my child, but she was grieved that his example of someone unsafe was people like his dad.

Our goal at Camp David is to help our campers to experience some of what having a caring father looks like and to give them a little picture of how their Heavenly Father loves and cares. On more than one occasion the little boys have called their camp counselor or other staff, "Daddy."

A counselor shares his thoughts about being a father figure: *"One of my campers (who was baptized this week) really opened up about how he felt when his dad went to jail and how Jesus helped him through that. It was a great experience to be a leader for these kids, and even like a father figure. I realized this when some of my campers told me that this was their first time going fishing or eating s'mores, and I was reminded of how my dad would do that with me when I was young. This made me see how blessed I was to have a great father. It was humbling to realize that God was using me to show these kids how God loves them as their Father." –John*

A movie that really impacted me this year was, "Gridiron Gang." As I watched the dilemma of young men getting out of juvie camp and being shot within days, my eyes were opened to another horror in the lives of our campers. About 70 percent of our campers are black. I know skin color makes no difference in God's eyes nor here at camp, but the reality is that it does make a difference in the lives of our campers.

Here are some facts that make me want to cry.

- **Seventy percent of black children live with no father**

- Black males ages 15-19 die from homicide at **46 times the rate** of white males their age.
- About **one in four black men** aged 20 to 29 **is in prison**, on probation or on parole—more than the total number of black men in college.
- Black men are nearly **seven times more likely to be incarcerated** with average jail sentences about 10 months longer than those of white men.
- The **unemployment rate** for black men **is more than twice** that for whites.

In my research I found that poorly educated, young black men moved in life patterns almost directly opposite to much of the rest of society. As urban crime rates are declining, incarceration rates for young black men are climbing.

Young black males are not born as criminals, prisoners or dropouts. But as they learn to walk and talk, something happens to push a large percentage of black men toward negative consequences, the sociologists say. The factors most cited as causes are fatherlessness, a pervasive negative entertainment culture, racism and multi-generational poverty that leave families without the tools to make a change.

While it is heart breaking to read these statistics, it is even harder when I can put faces to those numbers…boys like Marque, Latrell, Damion, Xavier … who have come to a week of camp but may have early deaths because they are caught in a cycle of crime, violence and poverty.

Another thing that stood out in the movie, "Gridiron Gang" was that all those young men had a common feeling. They felt worthless. Their father's rejection had deeply scared them. I realized that "feeling worthless" is a common feeling in the young men and women that come to our camp.

What can we do about this dilemma? What if these young men had people in their life tell them they are not worthless? What if someone showed them a different way of life, helped them have

Camp counselors may be the only "father" figure these kids experience

opportunities to become educated, employed, and to develop as leaders? What if someone who was walking with God could reveal to them a God that is NOT like their fathers? At Camp David, we introduce each of our young men and ladies to the unconditional love of God the Father, who does not see them as worthless.

Here is a story from Ben about one of our young black men, and the difference camp was making in his life. Ben wrote this at a time when we were just starting to launch a new program at camp, a program that we knew would have a great impact on campers...

"This summer I saw a camper growing from his hardships. He was a prisoner's son and had come the summer before as a camper. This year after coming as a camper we invited him back to a special staff training week for our older campers. While traveling to camp for the week of training, Donnell told my wife, Grace, about his cousin's tragic death under the wheels of a delivery truck a week before. This was just a sampling of his hardships. The first day of the training it was obvious Donnell had never learned to work. The next morning I sat on the front porch with Donnell and talked with him about his strengths and weaknesses, and setting goals. I encouraged him that he really had some great strengths that would help him go far in life, but there were also areas that he could grow in. We were able to work together to create some measurable goals for the week. To my amazement, each day I saw Donnell stepping up to the plate! By the end of the week, he had achieved all of his goals, and had literally become a working machine!

This year Donnell returned as a camper for the senior boys' week. As a camper, Donnell challenged an extremely laid-back, first-time camper, to memorize Bible verses. Together they tied for the most verses memorized! In fact, they set the new camp record for the number of verses memorized in a week of camp: a whopping 114 verses!

Donnell came back as a counselor for the next two weeks. He and his co-counselor inspired their whole team to memorize verses, and three of his campers won medals for the most verses! He went on to lead both of his teams those two weeks to win the wagon team challenges and set other new records. Donnell is learning to overcome; he is leading and doing a fine job at it. But what if Donnell and I hadn't had that talk on the front porch? What would have become of him? Or, better yet, what if we had been able to have talks and times together once a week?

The one key to helping a child grow through hardships is having someone there for them, someone they can tell their feelings to, someone to tell them they can make it, someone to inspire hope, and someone to reveal the Father God to them."

With our mentoring program, we have the chance to reveal the Father on a weekly basis, as in the next story.

Chapter 20

Just like His...

This is another article that Ben wrote in April 2012:

I held the door as seven year old Jared was carried out to the car, kicking and screaming. I remember thinking, "I hope he isn't old enough to come to camp this year!" Jared had come as a guest with his cousin, an alumni camper, to our 2009 Winter Camp Party, and Jared just didn't want it to end.

A couple of months later, we received Jared's camper application. I asked my wife, Grace, to tell his Aunt that with the difficulty we had at the camp party, I didn't think he was really ready for camp. Later that day, his aunt called. "Ben," she said, "Camp David is for kids like Jared. I mean if kids like Jared can't go, what's the point of camp?" That went right to my heart. She was right—Camp David was for kids like Jared! I asked God to forgive me and decided to give him a chance. To our surprise, Jared did great! A week of camp was just what he needed. Playing with the guys, eating with his counselors, and experiencing God's love made a big impact on him.

That fall, I visited a rundown, smoky row house with plastic on the windows to save on utilities. Jared's Aunt was sick, but welcomed me in as she talked about how much the kids loved camp. With his little cousin climbing on me, Jared's older cousin gave me the rundown on the family. "Jared's dad is getting out of prison next week." she said, matter of factly. "My baby brother's dad was just sentenced to prison so we won't be seeing him for a while. And mom's boyfriend... they picked him up yesterday for carrying drugs." Driving home after my visit, I thought of the statistics: if a prisoner's child is seven times more likely to end up in prison than his peers, Jared's future looked pretty bleak. All the men in his life were prisoners. Well, not all—not his counselors from camp! They were different. But would that be enough for Jared? Thankfully Jared has been able to come to camp each summer since then, and each year we see growth in him. Last summer, in 2011, Jared even made a decision to follow Jesus, and was baptized.

Last fall, I visited a supporting church and was surprised when Jared walked up to me. After saying hello, he jumped right into a story about scratching his neck while throwing a stick. I asked how one could hurt himself throwing a stick and the next thing I knew he was telling me about his aunt's boyfriend abusing him—definitely not your normal Sunday conversation! I was really caught off guard. Later I took Jared aside and told him that he did the right thing in talking about what had happened at home. He didn't deserve to be treated that way. When I got home, I made the necessary report to social services. When the social worker called me back she told me told me about the visit and how Jared held to his story, even correcting his Aunt when she tried to minimize the situation. My hope for Jared grew a little more because Jared had started to value himself.

When we started our Mentoring Program, Jared's cousin was matched with a mentor. Every week Jared would ask when he was going to get a mentor, and we hated telling him there was no guys available. In January, to our delight, we had a young man, an alumni counselor, contact us and ask to be matched with a camper—an answer to Jared's plea! This ambitious mentor, in his early twenties, gets together weekly with Jared. One of the things he taught Jared was how to change the oil in a car. In fact, Jared has now changed the oil in his aunt's car with his mentor's supervision! Jared lives each week now with the excitement and anticipation of spending time with his mentor—a man he looks up to, who loves God, cares about him, and is an engineering student. I don't know what Jared will do when he grows up, but I believe he's going to break out of that cycle of crime. I wouldn't be surprised if he pursues a degree in engineering, just like his...mentor."

Chapter 21

It's All About Relationships

A very important facet of camp is the bus ministry. Local churches partner with Camp David to bring the campers here and take them home again. One hot summer day, we got a phone call that the big van that was on its way from St. Louis to camp had broken down on the side of the road. There were about 18 little boys in that broken-down, hot van, and we knew we needed to send out a rescue team fast. My husband drove our family van, and several others on staff volunteered to drive so we could get all the campers back in several vehicles.

As you can imagine, the boys and the bus driver were very glad when Ben and the others drove up. We had the air conditioning running strong and were able to get them cooled down, but it seemed that the broken van incident had only heightened their excitement level about coming to camp. We have about 50 percent of our campers returning to camp each summer, and most of the ones in Ben's van were alumni campers. They were all talking, and asking questions and as my husband answered their questions, it stood out to him that there was a common theme in the questions. The kids weren't asking if we had made a bigger ropes course or gotten any new cool things at camp, all they wanted to know was, "*Is Grandpa Tom there?*" *Is my counselor from last year, Joel, there again?*" The thing they were looking forward to the most about camp was the people. Camp was all about relationships, and that was our goal. One of our core values is to have one counselor for every two (or three) campers. When a counselor only has to focus on two children, they can get beyond herding and policing the campers, to relationship building and mentoring.

Ben's Uncle Tom and Aunt Lillian first came to camp for a week in 2005. That was back in the days of the revival tent and outhouses. We were honored to have them come, and were even more excited when they told us they wanted to come again the next summer. At that point in our camp culture, everyone would choose a "camp name," just like Cliff and Susie did at their camp. So Ben's uncle became known at camp as "Grandpa Tom" and his aunt choose the name, "Grandma Pansy." The next summer they stayed for most of the weeks of camp. They had a heart to teach Creation through our nature class, and would take the campers on hikes in the woods and to the "Discovery Garden" where they would explain how God made each of those amazing plants. Grandma Pansy would pick some leaves of the herbs, or some fresh veggies in the garden, and offer them to the campers to taste. It was just a little alarming how many of the urban campers had no idea that food they had seen in the grocery store had actually been grown on a plant! We realized that the nature class was not only an opportunity to talk about *who* created everything; it was a hands on learning experience for *how* some food grows! Grandma Pansy has a funny story about one time when she pointed to the corn stalks and asked the boys what grew on them. One boy eagerly raised his hand, "*I know!! Pizza*!!" The next year we made sure we had some tomatoes, oregano, and basil in one of the raised beds, and we called it our "Pizza Garden!"

Grandpa Tom and Grandma Pansy have brought so much richness to the camp ministry as they have come each summer since 2005. Now Grandpa Tom drives a horse driven carriage for the Nature Hike, and the kids love his Clydesdale, Poka! Grandpa Tom is an artist, and he does this amazing "Chalk Talk" each week during camp. If you've never seen a "Chalk Talk," you will just have to visit summer camp during a Wednesday evening! Grandma Pansy not only writes the campers letters each day, and reads them bedtime stories, she prays for those kids every day of the year. And the kids know they are loved by this special couple. Last year I watched during lunch time as one of our troubled campers, who has been coming for about seven years, was finished eating. Instead of running outside to play carpet-ball, she just wanted to hang out at Grandpa Tom's table. She was used to his dry humor, and teased back a little. It hit me how so many things in this girl's life were dysfunctional relationally. Camp was one place where she could come away from the drama, and be loved by people like Grandpa Tom and Grandma Pansy. The relationships and love she experienced here at camp were why she kept coming back.

I asked Grandpa Tom what made them keep coming back when it was expensive and exhausting for a couple in their 70's to do so. Here is his response:

Grandpa Tom and Grandma Pansy come each summer to love on these kids.

"In 2005, we were in Mexico on a mission trip when I had a heart incident similar to a heart attack. But we had committed to a week at camp and we headed off to Missouri. The week was difficult but left us with a taste for more. We had previously worked on the streets of inner-city Chicago so we connected with the Camp David kids.

We returned to Michigan and I had a triple bypass heart surgery, but Camp David was impressed on our minds and *hearts. For most of our lives God has impressed us with the need to reach out to the "least of those among you." His command to give a glass of water, a meal, clothing, and to visit prisoners in jail has been a guide to ministry our whole lives. The children of Camp David provide that opportunity. While we do not visit in prison personally, we do so vicariously by coming alongside their children. James gives instructions to care for orphans and widows. In a practical way, most of Camp David's campers fit this category.*

Camp is difficult, tiring, long and usually hot. We probably could not be sustained if it were not for the changes we see year after year in the lives of those who return. Youth who started as campers 5, 6, or 7 years ago are now returning as staff and counselors."

When I talked to Grandma Pansy about why they come she said, *"It's the kids. I pray for those kids every day during the school year and it's so exciting to get to camp and see them again and see the changes in their lives."*

I love this story about a boy that Ben saw a change in—in just one week...

"Before he arrived, 11-year-old Ray was convinced that camp would be boring. He told his counselor, "At home I play video games all day. Camp is going to be one big bore." At the beginning of each event, there sat Ray with his this- is-gonna-

be-boring look. During fishing I found Ray sitting under a tree looking bored, while others excitedly caught sunfish and got pictures taken with their trophies. With some encouragement and coaching, I helped him catch fish and the photographers even got a few photos of him with a big grin. Wednesday, during swim time, Ray sat out, feeling sad because

It's not all that boring, really.

he couldn't reach his Mom on the phone, and he was afraid she was ignoring his calls (later he learned that she was in the hospital). His counselor, trying to make the most of the situation, got him started in a ping-pong game. Soon they were both laughing and having a good time. That night at the "Everybody's Birthday Party" the boys received footballs as gifts. Soon Ray and I were throwing his ball back and forth. He began to talk about his love of football and his aspirations. During the Ultimate Football game, Ray was positioned in the end zone, as to not aggravate his asthma. He made several great receptions and as we left the field, sweaty and tired, he drank in all the affirmation and belonging. In the cabin, as the boys were getting ready for bed, Ray opened up about his father's incarceration. His dad was in for "life plus

55 years" for his crime. Understanding this helped us to see a little more of the heart struggles this boy was dealing with. He had been so wounded by his parent's crime and incarceration which had completely changed his life, and it was hard to open up and trust anyone. The last night of camp during open mic time, Ray stood up and said, "Well, I made a lot of friends at camp. I didn't think I'd like camp, but I actually had a really good time, thanks to my counselors and new friends." Ray had experienced a new perspective on life. Making friends and building relationships was so much better than video games. This change in him was evident to everyone on staff.

Most importantly, Ray had made a decision to follow Jesus, who would never leave him or forsake him."

Chapter 22

No More Work

Things were changing. Most of the changes were very
exciting! After five years of using that little kitchen shack (and
cooking for up to 60 people from that tiny space) we finally
had our commercial kitchen working just in time for summer
camp 2009. No more carrying the food from the little shack
over to Ft. Turley for each meal! Our new kitchen had a large
work area, with three long countertops, food and dish storage
areas, and a dishwashing room. We did a fundraiser in the
spring of 2010 for a pre-owned commercial dishwasher, and
our staff were very excited when God provided the funds to
purchase it! There were still pots and pans to hand wash, but
the cups and plates were faster with the commercial unit!

The other huge improvement was that after five years of
using outhouses for seven weeks each summer, we finally had
our bathrooms finished!!! If you've never been without flush
toilets, you simply cannot imagine the excitement here at
camp when we could finally push that little silver handle and
the bathroom fixture would take care of the rest. I had fun

painting and decorating the bathrooms. The girls got bright colors and flowers on the walls, and the boy's bathroom was decorated with a fishing theme, since catching their first fish is the highlight of their week!

We were also able to finish the two staff housing rooms that were upstairs in the back of Ft. Turley, which provided housing for 20 staff! It took the help of a lot of friends working in the cold in January, and then a service team from Iowa helped in March with painting and laying carpet. Every detail of these improvements has its own story, from the carpet being very discounted by a local carpet store, to the paint being donated by Jazz Painting—a painter in the community who had extra cans!

Our numbers for camper attendance and volunteer staff were changing too, in fact in 2009 Camp David hosted 116 campers over seven weeks of camp, and had 96 volunteer staff!! Recruiting staff was becoming a huge job, as it took a lot of people working together to host camp for some of America's most at-risk kids.

By that point Camp David had hosted 470 campers over five years. We were sad to see the long list of kids that were eligible (they had a parent in prison), but we didn't have room for them. We were also maxed out with staff housing, so staff were sleeping in tents, and in neighbors' homes and were walking to camp each day. In the winter of 2009 we decided that if God would make it possible, we would begin construction on several new cabins. It was a huge bite to take for one year, but it all happened almost before we realized all that was going on.

The Catholic university student group in Rolla contacted us that fall and said they wanted to make Camp David their spring break mission project, and they would even raise funds towards the project! We had already drawn up plans to build a cabin for campers instead of building more covered wagons. While the covered wagons looked cool and added a western feel to camp, they were unsafe in thunderstorms, which meant whenever there was a big storm we would have to wake all the campers and counselors and have them move into Ft. Turley for the rest of the night. The little cabin was just the size project the university students were looking for and by early April they had our first cabin built. They named the cabin, "Newman Cabin," after their group.

Early that spring a church group contacted us and asked if they could bring a large team out for a day and help with a building project. Almost at the same time we received a call from Ben's Aunt Judy, who wanted to know how much it would cost to sponsor a camper cabin in memory of her father, Art Anderson. Things were happening so fast our heads were spinning! We were able to put Aunt Judy's memorial gift (which was for a large part of the project), and the church group together to build a second camper cabin that spring! This cabin was named the "Anderson Cabin" in honor of Aunt Judy's father. Having two new cabins enabled us to jump from four camper teams each week to six, and by the end of summer camp 2010 we had grown 50 percent in camper attendance!

The Newman Cabin was just one of three cabins built in 2010!

While God   was bringing together the details to these little cabins, He was also bringing together funds and volunteers to build a much larger cabin. Grandpa Tom had recognized the camp's need to have a tornado shelter, and he had become so invested in the ministry, that he was ready to make a significant donation towards a larger cabin that would include an office and bedroom for him and his wife. Not only that, but Grandpa Tom also talked to friends in Michigan who got excited about what God was doing and came down and framed in the new cabin on top of the concrete basement foundation!!

With all these changes to the grounds at camp, there was one thing that really needed to be changed in how we operated. When we started camp, Ben was running his own remodeling business, which was providing for our family. Then he began taking off the summers to do camp, which made finances tight, but as soon as camp was over, he'd knock on some doors and start bidding on new jobs again. As camp grew each year, it became harder and harder to juggle camp and remodeling work during the "off-season." Some weeks he'd go to the job site for three long days and then do camp work for three long days. Often while I was home at camp and Ben was on a remodeling job, people would call with questions, or issues would come up and I'd have to call him at work which added more stress. Finances became very tight with him only working part time, which was a big strain on our marriage.

Our family had sent out missionary letters to all our friends, and by October, 2009 we were at 81 percent of what we had set as the amount we could live on, but even then that was a very tight budget. While I was grateful for the generous support of so many friends and family, it was honestly a real struggle for me. There was no money for a family vacation. We were grateful for friends an hour away who allowed us to escape to their ministry house for a week where all we had to bring was our own food. Once camp was over we found it was important for the emotional health of our family to leave for a week and just recharge. A week or so after our ministry house vacation, I was teaching a Wednesday night girls' class at my church, and I asked the girls what fun things they had done over the summer. I was surprised how many had been to Disney World, or other amazing vacations and I'm ashamed to say, I felt the green jealousy bug come over me. If Ben and I both had good paying jobs we'd be able to offer lots of opportunities to our kids and be able to take nice vacations. But we were in ministry, and since we were crazy and started a camp, we had to live with the fact that there wasn't extra money. Several days later I was in the office, working on the sponsor cards and reading the campers' prayer requests.

A few that stood out to me were:

- "Pray that people would stop making fun of me at school" ~Austin
- "Pray for an easier life. I have a lot of rough times in my life. I only just now got a bed after a year of sleeping on the floor." ~Jade

- "Pray for my mom who is very sad because my grandfather passed away this January. Also pray for my father who has 8 years left in jail." ~Shae
- "Pray for my mom because she is in jail and I miss her."~ Adriel

Suddenly, I felt very blessed to have the privilege to be part of a ministry that was making a difference for kids. These kids were thankful for a bed, after sleeping on the floor. I remembered other stories from the camper's lives, and I knew the majority of them weren't thinking about Disney World. They were just wondering if there would be food in the house when they got home. (We've learned a lot of campers like water on their breakfast cereal...because they've never had it any other way!) Who was I to even taste that green bug of envy? I was soo rich. Not only did I have a home, and food on my shelves, but I had grown up in a Christian home, had my own Bible, and was educated so I could read it! I was able to serve in a ministry alongside my husband and children, and I had seen God's miraculous provision over and over. These are treasures that have no price on them— they are the kind that will last forever.

Sometimes even when we do have an attitude adjustment, we still need God to intervene. In our situation, God was working on my heart attitudes, but He also allowed Ben and me to be pushed up against a wall in order to have a change.

By the end of 2009, our community was really feeling the effects of America's recession. Many economists and Americans were calling the recession, "the worst economic crisis since the Depression." So when Ben bid on remodeling jobs that fall, with the same pricing he had always done, none of them took his bids. He would call old customers, and they would apologetically respond that they really didn't have any work, and things were tough. Having remodeling work dry up was extremely stressful to me, as I had to go grocery shopping each week for our family of six (soon to be seven!).

It was at the CCCA Ozark Region camping conference in the spring of 2010, that one of our board members and I attended a session about fundraising. I've been asked by other small camps if I feel the camping conferences are really helpful, and I always say, "Absolutely!" I am thankful Ben has really valued our annual regional camping conference and that he encourages our board members to attend, too. That session on fundraising in 2010 changed something huge for our family. As different camps talked about their methods of fundraising, one camp mentioned something that caught my attention. They had a policy that those on staff who did their fundraising, did not have to try to also raise missionary support for their families. They believed this would cause a conflict of interest. A *conflict of interest* looked like this to our family: making a presentation about the camp ministry at a church and having someone hand Ben a $100 bill and tell him to put it wherever it's needed most. Would he add that amount to our family Missionary Support, or would he put it into the General Fund for Camp David? Both had very real needs.

I am so thankful that board member Ron acted on what he had heard in that fundraising session, because at the next board meeting he spoke up. The CDO board ended up voting to finish out our missionary support, with the understanding that we would continue to do our best to raise funds for the camp. After six years of juggling two jobs, Ben was going to be able to focus on camp ministry, and with God's provision, he would actually receive a paycheck twice a month! I wept as I heard the news.

I had prayed, on my knees beside my bed, for years for God to provide our full missionary support. There were times in those years I wondered if He really heard me— times of silence when I felt like I needed an answer right then. When Ben came home from that board meeting and told me the news of the board's decision, I knew my Heavenly Father had heard my cries. I knew He had been teaching me to live on less, and to value the things that were eternal instead of those that would be destroyed by rust and greed. The name for God, "Jehovah-Jireh," had become very personal to me.

Chapter 23

Compassionate Community

We have camp insurance for injuries that happen at camp, but over the past nine years we have never had a major accident, and that is a miracle in and of itself. Our two big risk areas are the horses and swimming pool, but most of camp is "risky" and I believe it is prayer that has made a difference. From my father-in-law walking around praying during the summer, to our staff doing prayer walks around camp, it is a blessed piece of land. Many people tell us that as they drive past our welcome sign they feel a sense of peace over the camp.

Each year as camp grew and the number of staff on our team increased, so did frustrations increase! Staff training is usually the honeymoon period, where everyone on the team is new and everything is an exciting adventure. Then reality hits the first week of camp when the kids arrive and they keep you up half of the night, and one of your teammates start to push your buttons. By the third week of camp you are not only tired, you are sleep deprived and irritated at everyone else on the team.

That's how it was one Junior Boys' week. We were having 103 degree weather, and we were several weeks into the summer. Several staff had gotten sick, so we had to juggle people around and try to fill the empty spots. It was a VERY active group of boys and the counselors were worn out by Wednesday night. I had taken my little ones up to my house during evening chapel, and now they were tucked in their beds and sleeping soundly. I had headed back up to Ft. Turley in hopes that I could join the staff in a time of worship or a game. I was walking in the dark, but I was used to that. As I neared Ft. Turley, I saw some bright, orange lights on a vehicle that was parked out front. Without looking closely, I assumed it was Grandpa Tom's box-shaped truck, and thought maybe he had gone to town and come back and his truck was still running. When I got right up to the vehicle, I was shocked to discover it was NOT Grandpa Tom's truck, but an ambulance!! What was going on? Who was hurt? My mind and pulse started racing. I darted into Ft. Turley, which only had a few lights on, and there I saw what one of the most precious sights to me. Our staff were in a circle, holding hands and praying earnestly. Whatever the crisis was, they knew what was the most important. They were heroes in my mind at that moment.

But as Assistant Director, I really did want to know what was going on, so I stepped back out of the building and rushed over to the nurse's station. The old kitchen shack had been converted into a nurse's station, and as I got close I could see through the window that most of the activity was there. I couldn't really enter that crowded little room, but I signaled for a staff person to come over and fill me in on what was happening. It turned out that because of the terribly hot day, they had decided to let the campers do a rare thing and take a night-time swim. The boys were extremely excited about this opportunity, and went wild! While playing in the swimming pool, one boy got dunked a few times too many and started to choke. His counselor assisted him in getting out of the pool but after sitting on the swing for a few minutes, the boy said his chest hurt, and he was struggling to breathe. That's when someone panicked and called 911. Our Camp Nurse (an RN) was on the phone giving counsel to our resident CMA on what to do, but the call had already been made and in a few moments the ambulance was there. Ben had asked that they turn off their flashing lights and siren, and they had, which is why I didn't recognize their vehicle at first. The camper was taken to the hospital for a few hours for observation, but he was fine and was able to return to camp before the sunrise was complete.

That night when the staff had to join hands and unite in prayer, a change happened. It was a turning point for the entire summer. Instead of focusing on their differences and their expectations of what they wanted from camp, they had connected with the real reason they were all here—to be part of the work that God was doing, and to touch the lives of some really hurting kids. God became the center, and we became a true Christian community. Our key ingredient was compassion—for the kids, and for each other. If we can't show compassion and grace to each other when we make mistakes and when we wake up on the wrong side of the bed, we will never experience the fullness of what God wants in community.

Our staff devotional times grew richer after the night the ambulance was there. As a leadership team, we decided to become more intentional about engaging our staff and giving them opportunity to take the lead. We desired that each one would have the chance to share what God was teaching them so that we could all grow together. The small group prayer times grew richer because staff had taken off their masks and were being real with each other. And staff nights of worship were powerful. Those young people would enter His courts with thanksgiving and praise, and God's presence would fill the room. They wanted staff worship nights more than once a week, and it was hard to stop so we could go to bed.

I used to be skeptical of people who talked about "community" because it sounded like CONTROL. I knew what it was like to be controlled and judged, but camp ministry has provided me, and many others, a very real chance to experience Christian Community through His love and grace.

One of the ways this becomes personal for me is a little "project" we have among staff called, "Secret Agents." I have been the recipient of many encouraging notes from secret agents. I remember one day as I was standing in the lunch line, my mind was troubled thinking about the computers and printers that weren't working in the office. I had also just learned that I needed to find another counselor for the next week of camp. Suddenly, someone handed me a little, specially folded note. As I read the encouraging note, a lump formed in my throat and I realized that the little things that were frustrating me were small in comparison to what God was doing in my life. I delighted in the realization that someone was thinking and praying for me. I thanked my Father in heaven for the gift of community.

Here is a testimony about camp community, from an alumni staff: *"I think it's impossible to work at Camp David and not come away changed. I've worked here seven years—in many different capacities and jobs. Each one, every year, has taught me more about myself and God. The community of people that Camp attracts is one that is inherently growth-inspiring. I met most of my best friends at camp and every one of them has been impacted and challenged to grow here. I can honestly say that Camp David has been instrumental and even crucial in my development as a Christian." –Zhenya*

Chapter 24

Feeling Safe on a Horse

Do you know any little girls that love horses? As a little girl I had prayed for years for a horse, and when I was 13 my family moved to the country and my prayers were answered. I got my first horse!

When Ben and I started Camp David, we knew from the beginning we wanted horses to be an important part of camp. That first summer I walked campers around on a borrowed bay horse named, Faith, and gave horse rides. I loved the chance to talk one on one with each child. We had some very interesting conversations while they sat on the back of a huge animal! The next summer, our Food Service Director's daughter Linda, stepped into the "Horse Program Director" position, and she led the campers around on horses. Then Linda moved away for college, and she spent the next few summers working at large camps with their horse programs and at a large horse barn. Another friend, Ellie Hall, took the Horse Program director position for several years and did a great job.

In 2008, God led Linda to come back to our team as our summer Horse Program Director. Linda took ideas from all the things she had learned working at other camps as well as the horse barn, and reorganized our horse program to be more educational and to impact our campers in a much deeper way than we knew how to do before. Three years later, Linda graduated with a degree in Christian Education. Her dream was to use horses and discipleship to teach and impact kids. Ben and I realized that Linda's dreams fit right along with our dreams, and we invited her to join our team full-time! It was a very exciting day for us in January, 2011, when Linda accepted our invitation and became a full-time staff member! She was excited about the chance to put both her passions for horses and discipleship into practice as she served on our team at Camp David.

I would love to share a few of Linda's stories with you about horses and kids...

Each summer, our horse program reaches out and touches children of prisoners through challenges and accomplishments. If you have never stood right next to a 1,200 pound animal and had it put its' face in your face, you can't imagine the amount of adrenaline pumping through your veins. It is such a thrill to watch each summer as these kids conquer those fears and ride off as a team on their first trail ride. But these horses have also shown some of these kids a glimpse of love, acceptance, and respect that others in their life have failed to express. This is why I love using these majestic equines to teach kids, teens, and adults about the way God works with us!

There are so many types of horses in the world. We had one gelding this past summer who knew who he liked having around. Whenever an adult would ride him, they would end up so frustrated. But, these little campers with no riding experience would climb up on his back and come back with such joy. In fact, one young boy told us that he was only coming back if he could ride "his horse" again next year!

"I can do it!"

But my favorite memory of this horse was watching one junior girl climb down, give him his treat, and then throw her arms around his neck and say, "I love Roper. I just feel so safe whenever I'm on him!" It is at moments like these that I see God using these awesome animals to reach through the hurts and pains and show these kids glimpses of His love!

156/ Feeling Safe on a Horse

Taking some of America's most at-risk kids out on horseback can be eye-opening. On the surface, riding horses in the woods seems to lessen your awareness of the cultural differences you share, but there are moments when our campers give us startling insights into their home lives and culture. One such instance was during a horse ride where one of our mares, Beauty, was getting especially annoyed with our large Halflinger, Pippin. She had her ears laid back and her tail was swishing, warning him of the kick he would receive if he didn't back off and give her more space! As Wranglers, we warned the camper on Pippin's back to pull back on his reins so that Beauty wouldn't kick his horse.

He asked, "Why doesn't Beauty like Pippin?"

"Well, sometimes girl horses just don't like certain other horses. There isn't always a good reason," we explained.

Pondering our reply, his eyes lit up as he exclaimed, "I know why she doesn't like him!" We were rather intrigued as to why he thought the animosity existed and so we listened carefully.

"Pippin and Beauty used to be married and had a girl, Rosa (another mare at our camp). But they divorced, and Pippin got to keep Rosa in the divorce and now Beauty hates Pippin!"

This was such an eye opener to the pain, separation, and constant change in the lives of such young campers. This young boy wasn't over 11 years old and yet he had seen so much divorce and family disruption that it translated into how he interpreted a mare's dislike of a certain horse.

Although each summer has its stories, there are some moments that have stuck with me forever. Many of our campers struggle with fear and trepidation as they approach these huge, hooved animals. One such girl was finally convinced to mount up, only to discover just how high up you feel on top of a horse. She was very nervous, and I just encouraged her to let me lead her horse in a circle while she held on up there. Shaking a bit, she conceded—gripping the saddle horn with white knuckles. Her face was tense, and after a few steps I told her to pull back on her reins and say, "Whoa." Hesitantly, she pulled and quietly said, "Whoa." The horse—Rosa, an old faithful mare who always takes care of scared kids—stopped immediately. At that moment, the smile that exploded on that girl's face was priceless as she exclaimed, "She listened to me!" I realized this might be one of the few times in her life that she was in control of a situation that seemed beyond her.

That was four summers ago. She rode out on the trail that summer on her faithful steed, and every summer after that she would exclaim that Rosa was her favorite, and the only horse she could ever ride. Then the eventful day happened last summer. She was there for a week of camp, and Rosa had to have the week off because of an injury. At first, this camper refused to ride, claiming that she only felt safe on Rosa and wouldn't go out on any other horse. After some coaxing and explaining, she agreed to try a horse named Rylee at the barn. She climbed on board and was again shocked at the height because Rylee was quite a bit taller than Rosa, but she braved on through and went out on the trail. It was so amazing to see how the steps taken four summers ago helped her overcome a new fear of horses—riding a different horse! This girl may never become a cowgirl, yet she learned a lot about trust, courage, and overcoming fears on the backs of God's majestic equines!

You know your staff are here for ministry to kids, and not for the amazing facility—when there is no facility! Ellie and Linda, our Horse Program Directors, both made do without all the niceties of a typical horse program. Not only did we NOT have a riding arena, nice pastures, or lots of horse stalls—we didn't even have a barn!! After a few years, Ben rescued an old shed from a remodeling job. It was only 6'x6' which is smaller than your typical bathroom! A service team painted the shed "barn red," and the Horse Program took it over by building saddle racks on the walls, and putting a tote with riding helmets on the floor. This was our "Horse Barn" for two summers. Looking back, our Horse Program Directors had a lot they could have complained about, but they didn't. To everyone's excitement though, in the spring of 2011, we began a new building for a Horse and Maintenance barn. This was our first building project that we actually raised the money and then hired someone else to build a pole building for camp. It was so much less stressful for our family that Ben didn't have to build it all, and it also went up super-fast!

The new 30'x46' building is a huge blessing! It includes a maintenance area to store tools and building supplies, horse stalls, a tack room, and a long overhang that the horses can stand under to get shade. We were blessed to have a church group come out and put in all the electric, which wasn't covered by the contractor. This means the new building has our

The new horse barn is 30 times larger than the old shed!

trademark—being built by the hands of many different volunteers who came out and helped bring it to completion. The man who shoes our horses even brought a team out to put up a fence for a new paddock for the horses next to the new barn.

While our campers were learning they can be safe on the back of a large horse, we were learning to trust our Heavenly Father to provide for all our needs- and He did!

Chapter 25

Saved in Abstinence Class

Deciding to have an abstinence class as one of our morning rotations for senior camper weeks was easy when we realized that around 50 percent of our senior campers (ages 13 to 16) were already sexually active. For many, the idea of saving sex for marriage was totally out of their box. They couldn't believe we would suggest such an idea. There were others who were overwhelmed with guilt and shame for what they had done. In the abstinence class, Camp Director Ben shares with the boys how God created sex as his special way of bonding two people together in a lifelong covenant. He also talks about how lust turns sex into an addiction that has nothing to do with relationship and everything to do with creating a bigger high, which leaves them feeling shameful and alone.

Another issue is how lust turns girls into objects of lust. Most of the boys have never considered how it affects girls. While Ben does go over the truth about STD's and the negative effects of multiple sex partners, he wants our campers to learn healthy ways to deal with their desires. Telling our campers they just shouldn't have sex is like telling them to not eat ice cream. But when we help them get in touch with their feelings and their desire for love or acceptance, we can help them explore healthier and more meaningful ways to have their needs met.

Not only was the camp office in my home, the "conference/meeting room" was, too. So for each abstinence class, my living room was filled with senior campers sitting all over my couches with serious expressions on their faces. It was very uncomfortable for our staff girls who needed to walk through the living room to get to the camp office while one of THOSE classes was being conducted! One morning during a boys' week, it seemed like there was some extra noise in the class. We couldn't figure it out from inside the office, but we weren't about to peek in and see what was going on. I did ask Ben about it after lunch. "Oh," he said with a big grin, "two boys got saved this morning during abstinence class!!" Now that would make a good church testimony: "I was saved in an abstinence class!" It was not the only time campers met their Maker during that special class in my living room.

This is one of my favorite stories Ben titled, *A Daisy Begins to Bloom*.

"When I came, I knew this was a Christian camp. I had decided that I wouldn't sing or be part of any of the Christian stuff. I

hated God and I hated men... For the past nine months I broke every one of the Ten Commandments, except do not murder..."
This was part of an honest confession from Daisy, during the last "What About It" class. In the class we talked about relationships, abstinence (and sex), broken people, and meeting our need for love in healthy ways. Daisy, a timid 15-year- old girl, had spent 12 long years in an isolated and hopeless home situation where she and her siblings were regularly abused. If ever a person had a reason to be bitter, she did. Daisy was here for the senior girls' camp, notoriously the most difficult week of summer. The camp theme for this summer was "Darkness to Light" and how being honest about "who we really are" dispels the darkness and brings light into our lives. As the week progressed they really began to open up. Though only 13 to 16 years of age, these girls shared about abortions, abuse, drugs, crime, cutting, sexual confusion, gangs, and much heart ache. What touched these girls was that though very few of the counselors had experienced the campers' pain, they unconditionally loved them.

The last morning of the "What About It" class, after honestly sharing her darkness, Daisy asked me (I was teaching with another lady staff) what she should do if she wanted to follow Jesus. She wanted to come to Jesus but wasn't sure He would accept her because of how she had hated Him and tried to hurt Him. She was deeply moved to learn that God still loved her. Jesus understood her pain and He was still more than willing to *forgive her for everything she had done wrong. Sitting there on the couch, Daisy prayed and accepted Jesus as her Savior, right there in front of all her fellow campers. The last day of camp Daisy was beaming with joy as she continued to grasp the immeasurable love God had for her. Just before she got in the car to leave camp, Daisy asked me for a hug and said, "**Thanks for helping me see that not all men are bad.**"*

When discussing issues about abstinence with girls, one thing that comes up is abortion. We have the amazing opportunity to share about the value of life, including unborn babies, with teenage girls. We learned a few years ago from a camp counselor, that one of her campers had been asked to go with a friend to have an abortion. At camp this young lady had learned about the value of life for unborn babies, and she was able to stand strong and refused to go with her friend.

Even though we know many of our campers are already sexually active, it was still a shock the Monday that our senior girl campers arrived and we learned that one of the 15 year old girls was pregnant. In talking with Papa Big Heart, this young mama said that she was going to abort her baby because there was no one to care for her baby, and no one would love her baby. The "no one" seemed to include herself— which is surprising until you understand the home she comes from. This girl has known so much drama in her home that she struggles to receive love, and give it away. A friend, who has served as a counselor at some local pregnancy centers, came out to camp to spend time talking with our camper. After learning about the reality of abortion, and adoption as an option, our camper seemed to change her mind to consider other options. Sadly, she is so unstable we really don't know what will happen over the next few months. This young girl says her mom has told her, "If you get pregnant, I will kill your baby." This story is not over yet, but we are reminded of how important these campers (and their children) are to God's heart. I am so grateful that we had not only the opportunity to touch this young lady's life, but hopefully the life of her baby too.

Chapter 26

Learning Forgiveness

When tall, heavy-set Destiny arrived at camp, her only shoes were her flip flops. She came with other things though—wounds from a gang that jumped her in her neighborhood just days before. Destiny was only thirteen years old, but she looked much older and was a little intimidating with her tough exterior.

The senior girl campers often bring adult counselors to tears. To protect their tattered hearts these girls often become catty, spiteful, guarded, scoffing bullies. It is a very emotional and draining week for the counselors. To love these teenage girls requires all the grace of God.

The night before the campers arrived we broke into six groups and walked all over camp praying for the girls that would be coming that week. "Prayer Walking" had become a tradition that started after the really difficult senior girls' camp two years before! As the buses arrived the next day, there was cheering as the campers were welcomed to camp. One teen later confessed, "*I expected the prissy white girls to*

be in one group, the black girls in another and then there would
be me, but when the doors opened… it was like they were giving
me a big hug." That is our desire—that our campers would
feel loved as soon as they enter our doors.

Most of the girls that week came from the 'hood.' Many had
never been out of their part of the city, and when they had
received the invitation to a free week of camp they saw it as a
way to get away from their reality. Some of the girls said that
the beds in the wagon cabins (a piece of plywood with a 4"
thick mattress on it) were better than the beds they had at
home. Some said they really just lived in the streets because
there was no place for them at home. And they all loved the
food at camp—three hot meals a day, for four days was like
heaven.

But as the week progressed, there was a girl-fight brewing.
Tension was on the rise, and by the last evening of camp it
was obvious to me when I walked down to the campfire circle.
The black girls were all sitting together on one side of the
circle, and the counselors and a few white campers were on
the other side (It's usually a ratio of 7:3 with black and white
campers.) To tell the truth, I was even scared. This had never
happened before, and the tension in the air was so thick you
could have sliced it with a knife.

As the campfire time started, Ben asked the campers to move
around the circle and sit as teams with their counselors.

Thankfully, they did, but the looks they shot our team weren't very friendly. We actually got through the character awards time. There was more laughing (borderline mocking) than usual, and it felt like a cover-up for the tension in the air. After the awards time, I headed home with my little ones, and that's when the fight broke out.

A group of girls approached Destiny, and when she tried to push past to get away, a girl spat in her face. Destiny quickly threw her to the ground and began kicking her.

Thankfully, our Leadership Team is trained each year in *Managing Aggressive Behavior*, and seconds later they stepped in and separated the girls, which stopped the fight. But it took a long time before the campers were emotionally settled that night. Here is camp counselor Paula's story about the night of the fight:

"Within five minutes after the campfire time was over and my campers were inside our wagon, a real fight broke out with campers in another team. As the Leadership Team stepped in, everyone was sent to their wagons with their camp counselors. What really stood out to me was how my campers reacted to the fight. In our cabin my girls were hysterical, yelling profanity, and crying. The reason? Because they couldn't understand how those other girls could be that disrespectful towards what had been offered to them at this camp. They said things like, "Papa Big Heart puts his entire family and baby into

this; and you, Paula, could be somewhere on a vacation with your family. The other counselors give up their summers to be here too." "I came here to get away from home and my neighborhood, to get away from the fighting, and they bring it out here!" "Most of us are going back to sleeping in worse conditions than the mats on the wagons, and to getting beat on by our mamas."

My sister (a camp "Auntie") came to check on our wagon and the girls said, "We are so sorry, Auntie Ellen, we are so sorry." My sister said, "Did you start the fight? Were you in the fight?" They continued to ask for forgiveness. They were asking for forgiveness for being black and from the inner city. One of the campers even said, "Ms. Paula, if I could change the color of my skin to white, I would." They couldn't understand how we could be forgiving, and accepting, and give up our lives to be there for them. God opened the door to share the love of Christ through the aftermath of the fight."

In the middle of the crying and upheaval, the campers began to open up to their counselors more than ever before. One counselor wrote: *"My girls opened about the horror that they live in, things that I've never imagined any 14 or 15-year-olds even knowing about. In tears, they said things like, "The street is our father, until you go to jail. Then, you are alone in this world." "I've never had a chance. I was 6 the first time I was raped. How can God forgive me?"* This opened the door to share about God's amazing love and forgiveness. There was so much pain in their hearts that we couldn't "fix," but we could love.

Our staff stayed up very late that night meeting with the campers involved in the fight, and tried to teach steps for conflict resolution. Destiny was pulled out of her team, mostly for her own safety, and stayed with the Counselor Coach. In discussion over what had happened, Destiny stated, "*This always happens to me, no matter where I go. That's why I don't trust anyone.*" It is hard to see a girl so hurt by others that she can't trust anyone. Papa Big Heart talked to her about how to forgive, different ways to deal with conflict, and how to be a peacemaker. We made special arrangements for her to be driven back to St. Louis separately from the other girls as we didn't want another fight to start on the bus ride back. Destiny came back to camp the next summer. As she stepped off the bus we were pleased with the change in her. She smiled at the staff, and the chip on her shoulder was gone. She seemed to have learned some steps to being a peacemaker. We even watched Destiny walk away from an argument with another camper that second year, and we praised her for choosing a different way to deal with conflict.

Sometimes when campers learn conflict resolution and how to forgive, they end up making new friends. Here is a story from Mark, a junior boy counselor.

"I had a camper dealing with a lot of pain and anger. Mom and Dad were both in jail for selling meth, and the grandfather who he lived with was an abusive drunk. He had a conflict with another camper which brought to the surface a lot of pain and anger. After talking with him and the counselor coach, he worked through the conflict, forgave the camper with whom he had the conflict, and became one of his best friends. The conflict showed me the real pain these campers are experiencing in their home lives. He gave me hugs all morning on Friday before he left and was sad to go. It was a privilege for God to allow me to be his counselor and be a positive male role model in his life, and to express how he has his Father in heaven by his side at all times."

Chapter 27

The Good News

Did you ever bake muffins, and forget the baking powder? They end up flat! If I didn't talk about the ingredient in our ministry that makes the biggest difference, all the time and effort we had put into having birthday parties and personalized photo albums would be flat, useless. Mark 8:36 says, *"What good is it for someone to gain the whole world, yet forfeit their soul?"*

The Good News is that despite all our selfishness, greed, pride, and the hurtful things we have done, God has offered us a clean slate—forgiveness and life with Him in heaven is a gift. He doesn't look at the statistics, or what my parents have done (or have not done). He doesn't offer this gift of salvation only to those who haven't punched anyone out. It is a free gift to those who will admit they've done wrong, and that they need God. And that is really good news. I don't have to be perfect for God, or earn my salvation. I love the simplicity of this— Jesus is THE way, THE truth, and THE life.

Many people ask us, "How many campers are getting saved at your camp?" That is a hard question to answer. The Gospel is clearly presented each week, but we don't know all that God is doing. Our goal is not to get a whole lot of decisions for Christ at camp, per say. But rather to introduce them to Jesus and the exciting Good News of what He has done. Whether or not they believe and receive the gift is a work of God in their hearts.

Another struggle is that most of our campers never go to church, so the only time they learn about God is once a year at camp and sometimes it takes years to see the seeds that have been planted take root. Last year we did have many more decisions for Christ than in previous years: out of 202 campers, 53 made decisions for Christ! I know that many of those campers had been coming for years, but last year everything came together in their hearts and understanding. When they made their decision, it really was life-changing.

How do you make the Good News understandable to a child? There is this little book that we use and what is so unique about it is that there are no words in this book. It is just pages of solid colors. Simple enough for a child to understand.

At age 16, I took a week of training with Child Evangelism Fellowship to become one of their summer missionaries. My friend Elizabeth took the training with me, and we were both impressed with this little book that they used to share the

Gospel. Although I had grown up in a Christian home and gone to church my entire life, it wasn't until that week of training that I really learned how to share my faith.

What a joy each summer to be able to teach our counselors how to use this little "Wordless" book with the five different colored pages. Each color represents an important key to understanding the Gospel message, for example:

BLACK – Sin; Romans 3:23 "All have sinned…"
RED – Blood; I John 1:7 "Jesus' blood covers all sin"
WHITE – Pure; Psalm 51:7 "Jesus washes away confessed sin"
YELLOW – Heaven; John 14:2 "Believe on Jesus and receive Eternal Life"
GREEN – Grow; 2 Peter 3:18 "Grow in the knowledge of the Lord"

When I read the counselors' testimonies at the end of each week of camp, my heart feels like it wants to burst. I am so blessed to be part of a ministry that gives Christian young people the opportunity to share their faith, and see children receive God's gift of salvation. It is life-changing for them.

Here are a few of their stories…
"During the week several of my campers were having trouble concentrating. Tuesday night, I had the chance to share the Wordless Book with them. At first they were struggling to concentrate. But then, as I told them about how their sin separates them from God, you could tell it was starting to click.

And as I got to the 'clean' page, instead of being hyper and distracted, all of their energy and focus was on praying to receive salvation. And they were more than ready to pray before I had even finished explaining what they should include in their prayer! That night, I got to see two wonderful young ladies enter the family of God!" –Melissa Bergthold

"It was really special to see one of my campers really "get" the Gospel message. She was on the verge of tears after Monday night's message when she realized that she had to be perfect to go to heaven. She pleaded with me to tell her how God made a way for us to go to heaven despite our sin and afterwards she exclaimed, "Ohh, He's so nice! I want to pray and thank Him for doing that right now!" Throughout the rest of the week, she had lots of good, deep questions about salvation and on Wednesday night she asked me to help her receive Jesus' gift of salvation. Seeing the Holy Spirit work in her life like that was a treasure I'll always cherish." –Abigail Greek

"This week I got to lead one of my campers to Christ. It was my first time to ever lead anyone to Him. It was pretty cool! We were going through the Wordless Book and she kept asking "So, how do I do it? How do I accept Christ?" I kept telling her "Just a second, I'm getting there." She was sooo excited about it. After we had finished I was telling her that God had adopted her as His daughter and that she was now a Princess, a daughter of the King of Kings. Later that night, Auntie Marilyn was reading

my girls a bedtime story and it was talking about how true princesses were the Daughters of God. My camper looked at me and said, "That's what you were telling me!" I was so pleased to realize that she had understood!" –Laura Marchbank

"The night we shared the gospel with our campers several accepted Christ, and one who accepted Christ and got baptized just was so happy and excited about it. It made everything worth it. It was so wonderful to see their faces light up at the mention of their baptism or of Jesus." –Abby Hall

"During the time to share the gospel, both girls I was working with were very interested, wanting to take in every word. Both were always bubbly until this point when they got very serious and announced that they wanted to accept Jesus. These two girls showed me that even though they were young they too could follow a loving God. Both began to show more enthusiasm at devotions and I saw a change in the way they worshipped. Both girls joyfully embraced whatever they could to learn more about God. After each girl accepted Jesus, she listened attentively to the Bible and requested it to be read when available. The hope and love God gives washed over these two almost immediately. The change in their manners was astounding." –Hannah Beck

"I now firmly believe that the best feeling to experience is that of seeing a young life choose to follow Jesus Christ."- Ian Nail

In the story of the woman who washed Jesus feet with her hair, the religious leaders of that day criticized the woman for pouring expensive perfume on Jesus' feet. But Jesus responded by saying, "*I tell you, her sins—and they are many—have been forgiven, so she has shown me much love. But a person who is forgiven little shows only little love.*" (Luke 7:47)

Our campers know they have been forgiven much. They also love much.

Sharing the Good News

Chapter 28

Bold Love

Here is an article Ben wrote in November of 2010:

I can still remember sitting by little Xavier with his short curly hair and teary brown eyes. He was telling me about a fight he saw in his home that ended with a gunshot and police cars. As I remember it today I want to say fortunately, no one was hurt; but someone was hurt—Xavier. His childhood was rocked to the core with the realization that, in a moment, people he loved could be killed in an angry fight. Then I think of our senior girl campers who have been hurt in ways worse than I could ever imagine. What is the future for these children? Without someone to show them a different way to live, they too will become parents of children just like them, and the endless cycle of crime, prostitution, gangs, and drugs will continue.

Over a half a century ago five men flew deep into the jungles of Ecuador on a bold mission to save a group of people, called the "Aucas," who were trapped in a cycle of killing that was rushing them toward annihilation. In a final attempt of bold love the five men refused to retaliate as they were speared to death by members of the very tribe they had come to save. Two and a half years later the "bold love" lived on as a sister, wife, and young daughter went back to the Auca people to continue the mission of God's love and forgiveness. Overwhelmed by their love, the Aucas began to change and put their faith in Jesus. The killing stopped and today the Auca people have grandparents. This was something they never had before.

As the story of this "bold love" has spread, thousands of people have dedicated their lives to share the love of Christ with those who have never heard. At eight years of age, my mother was one of those young people. The "bold love" story has affected me as well. However, "bold love" did not start with the five missionaries. It began long before—when Jesus, the creator of the world, came to earth. Jesus willingly paid with his own life for our freedom from sin and death. As I look at the volunteers who serve at Camp David, I see this same "bold love." Unpaid, they give up large portions of their summer to love some very difficult children.

I remember one night at camp, the boys were particularly difficult to get to sleep, and it was late before all was silent. Checking the last wagon, I whispered a good night to the counselor and, as I walked away, I pondered what it was that kept bringing him back. He knew about the non-air-conditioned cabins, late nights, the bugs, and the emotional energy drain the boys can be. I concluded that it had to be this "bold love." It was something that, once he tasted, he had to taste again.

There are many people working together to make camp a reality for the campers. People like two sisters, ages 11 and 16, who keep a jar on their kitchen counter which they fill with their own money to send campers to camp. They have almost collected enough to sponsor a second camper for this year. Or the numerous prisoners who send $3 or $4 donations every month from their limited income. People like a young married couple, who decided to sell their motorcycle and volunteer an entire summer at camp. We recently received a donation from a woman whose widow friend arranged to sponsor a camper by giving her monthly installments for the next three months. There was also a stay-at-home mom who put on a garage sale and used the proceeds to sponsor a camper.

They remind me of the story of the little boy who gave five loaves and two fish to Jesus, who then fed over five thousand. These people have given out of what they have, and as a result they discover the joy of seeing God at work. The people who make a camp like ours possible are rarely those with huge salaries. They are people like you and me who are willing to step out in faith and give.

Let's give our lives to boldly loving the "unlovable."

Chapter 29

Wives of the Incarcerated

I was at a special conference for those involved with Angel Tree and Prison Fellowship. While I enjoyed all the workshops and everything I was learning, I was the most excited about meeting Mary Kay Beard, the founder of Angel Tree. Mary Kay had such a sweet spirit and love for people; it was hard to picture her as a hardened criminal in her early days! After she spoke, I was excited to purchase a copy of Mary Kay's book, *Rogue Angel.* Her story opened my eyes and heart for the mothers of our campers.

I am so grateful for the Angel Tree program that Mary Kay started, which has grown to two main outreaches. The first is "Angel Tree Christmas" where churches help to provide Christmas gifts on behalf of inmates to their children. The second outreach is "Angel Tree Camping" which is vital to our camp ministry. We are a registered *Angel Tree Camp,* which enables them to send us a long list of children in our service area that we can contact and invite to camp.

Between sessions where Mary Kay and others spoke of the needs of prisoners' families, I visited with those at my table. I learned that the lady sitting next to me had recently had her husband get out of prison. This was actually my first time to get to know a woman who had experienced having a husband incarcerated, and what she shared was eye-opening for me. Her husband was having a really hard time finding work now that he was out of prison, so he stayed home with their kids while she worked. Since she had raised their children for so many years while he was behind bars, there was now friction between them as they tried to parent their children together. But the thing she mentioned that stood out the most, was that while her husband was in prison, she had never been able to get settled into a church. As soon as people in a church found out that her husband was a prisoner, their attitudes toward her would change drastically. In a short time she would move on to try to find a more welcoming place where she and her children could worship God. She even said that when visiting churches she learned to respond to questions concerning her husband by saying he was in the military, fighting overseas, since that was acceptable in society. My heart ached for this mom, and all the other moms who deal with the severe judgment society places on prisoner's wives. The social stigma for these women is worse than those who are widowed or divorced.

Through reading, *Family Arrested*, by Ann Edenfield, my eyes were more opened to the struggles wives of the incarcerated experience. Here is Ann's perspective on how her husband's incarceration affected their family: "*In essence, our whole family was arrested* (she had 4 young sons). *We were stopped in our tracks. We weren't handcuffed and hauled off to prison, but our whole family structure was thrown into chaos. My husband's incarceration affected all of us in very significant ways. My family was suddenly ostracized from much of what we had known and counted on. It felt like we had invisible bars surrounding us, and many people, including friends, did not want to get near us. We were a FAMILY ARRESTED.*"

Some of Ann's stories of how society responded to her, after learning of her husband's incarceration made me angry. Not only did her insurance agent, a long time family friend, refuse to insure her anymore, but she was rejected over and over by other insurance companies. She learned to be very creative about how she explained where her husband was! The story that especially got me was how Ann's church family turned their backs on her when her husband was arrested. Thankfully a friend introduced Ann to another pastor, who was very supportive of her and her sons during her husband's incarceration. Ann was able to be actively involved with this church for the next six years, at which time the church got a new pastor. When the new pastor learned that her husband was going to be getting out of prison soon, he said he would no longer be her pastor. The new pastor's harsh words were devastating for Ann.

I am thankful our pastor has a real heart for prison ministry, and has been supportive of our church being involved with Angel Tree Christmas for many years. One year I suggested that we try to have a party at the church and invite the Angel Tree families out, instead of delivering the gifts to their individual homes. What happened at the party gave me another glimpse of life for the wives of the incarcerated. We actually only had two families come to the big Christmas dinner we had prepared. But the two moms that did come with their children sat at the same table together. I watched as they began to talk. They asked which prison each other's husband was in, and then started to open up about different challenges they were facing. They used terms in talking about their husband's prison lives that were unfamiliar to me, but they understood. I could tell that for each of those ladies having someone who understood what they were talking about and going through was the best gift we could have given.

Churches often offer fantastic programs for moms of preschoolers, and support groups for single moms, but moms whose husbands are incarcerated usually just stay away from churches. In fact, because of the shame and social stigma that comes with having a spouse incarcerated, they usually stay isolated in our society altogether. A challenge that comes with these women being isolated in society is there is no one to defend them. When they receive fines and letters from the IRS, credit companies, or landlords, they don't know who to turn to for help. They really need someone to help them walk this dark road.

My dream is to begin a program over the next five years—a Support Group/Network for the moms of our campers. Just as their children come to camp, and experience for the first time the sense of community around an issue in their lives, I want these moms to be able to connect, and to have a safe place to be real and to be loved on. Some of these moms will need mentors, some will need parenting classes, but all will need a place that is free from the shame of having a family member incarcerated.

I think the only thing that is worse than feeling shamed because of a mistake your spouse made, is seeing your children suffer the shame of their daddy's mistake and not being able to do anything to protect your children from the rejection they face in society. Here is a letter from one of our campers' moms several years ago. Her boys were some of our first campers...

*"Hi, My name is Laura, and my children, Matt and Zach, are past campers at Camp David. This has been a great opportunity for my children. They look forward to the coming summer and what they are going to experience. They have a hard enough life as it is, so being able to get out of town for a week that is totally dedicated to them is the best gift. They come home from camp having learned several new things and have pictures and notes, and they really feel cared for and have become part of the Camp David Family. From my point of view, it is comforting for me to know this is a **safe and non-judgmental place for the boys to go**. They learn so many things about God and good Christian values that will follow them through life. Statistics for these children are stacked against them. **Even in this day and age, prisoner's families are not treated fairly all the time. There are some people that look badly on the innocent children because of a mistake that was made by a loved one.** I will never be able to say enough good things about this ministry and how it has so positively affected our lives. They send out monthly newsletters and I can see all the joy and fun they had all year long. Please*

Each camper goes home with photo album pages of their fun times at camp!

don't let this ministry fade away. It is so vital to these children. **This is a safe place for children to go to when they may not live in a safe place the rest of the year.** *This is something so special for them."*

❧

Here are a few more testimonies from the moms of our campers. The ways camp affected their children give us more insight into the lives of families of the incarcerated.

"My son had a blast at camp! Everything they did made him feel special. The fishing, archery, horseback riding and attention he received made him really happy. Following camp he had a better understanding **that he wasn't the only one without a dad. I think he appreciated me even more after camp. I feel he came home more confidant and sure of himself."** K.M.

"Camp David was absolutely GREAT for my son. **He has had a difficult time making friends in the past and he took a giant step in that area during his week** *stay. He treasures the staff and the photos of the time he spent at Camp David."* S.C.

"My boys loved that Camp David gave them the chance to get away from the drama and negative people in their daily lives. *Camp helped them be more at peace. They really had a hard time last year, but they have calmed down."* K.S.

"*My daughter loved the horseback riding, petting zoo, and basically any animal you have!! She LOVED the counselors, Grandpa & Grandma, and the Princess Dinner was a big hit. When Rachel got home she couldn't wait to share about her baptism.* **It was really great to hear her pride and self-confidence as she told of her new friends and I could tell she enjoyed it so much.** *I think the binder with pictures from camp was just WONDERFUL! Transportation is also a wonderful thing you all provide. My husband has been in prison for 8 years and* **there just isn't much support for the kids.** *We are truly blessed she was able to attend. Thank you so much!*"
B.W.

Campers love our huggable petting zoo animals!

Chapter 30

I Can't Do It Anymore

I really believed in the Camp David ministry. But I was worn out. It's one thing to stretch yourself out for a short period of time, but extended seasons of overload cause burn-out. When we started camp I only had two little girls, but now I had four children, and I was homeschooling three of them. And as the ministry grew, so did the office work. Over the years I had learned to do graphic design and create newsletters, make promotional DVD's and I even designed the "face" of our new website. But all that took a lot of time—and late nights. Even if I had worked 40 hours a week, I wouldn't have been able to keep up with the office work. I did have a lot of volunteers come out. Some came out on a weekly basis, others were on call for extra busy times. But the inconsistency in the volunteer help was creating a problem in the office, and the burden of that load was resting on my shoulders.

In the fall of 2009, we discovered that we were expecting baby number five. I will share more later about that, but dealing with morning sickness and pregnancy on top of my already too full plate, really pushed me over the edge. And the story of how God provided was really amazing.

A generous donor had created a fund to help with the professional development of the camp director, my husband. So in April 2010, Ben registered to attend the Christian Leadership Association conference in California. While I was excited for Ben that God had provided for him to be able to go to the conference and get away for a little, I was also in my last trimester of pregnancy and feeling very overwhelmed with camp. Shortly before the day he flew to San Diego, our family van broke down—the transmission went out. Thankfully, my brother Dave loaned us his van until we could find a new one, which we drove to the airport that spring day to drop Ben off.

Before we got to the airport, we went to a restaurant for lunch together as a family (a rare treat) but very needed in light of all the busyness. I was surprised that my seven-year-old son, Timmy, wasn't real hungry at the restaurant as that was uncharacteristic of him. But I dismissed it and tried to focus on the last few moments I was having with my hubby before he left for several days.

After our delicious lunch, we headed to the airport and since we were early, we talked more in the waiting area. Suddenly Timmy jumped up and said he had to run to the bathroom. He only made it half-way there before he started to vomit in the hallway. Oh no! Ben kindly cleaned up Timmy for me, but by then they were calling his flight on the loudspeaker and the next thing I knew, Ben was running to catch his plane. I told Timmy to keep a bag in his hand and got my troupe together to head for the van. As we left the airport parking lot we saw Ben's plane getting ready for take-off, and we pulled to the side of the road and rolled down the windows to watch. I'm sure Ben couldn't see us waving, but it was fun for the kids to see his plane take off. As we got back on the road, we tried to put the windows back up in Dave's van, but they didn't work. After calling and learning it had never been a problem before, we prayed, but the windows would not go back up. It was a two-hour drive home, and I didn't know how we'd do it with the windows completely down. But that was the only thing to do— head home with the windows open, especially since Timmy was at it again in the back seat. I guess God knew the smell would have been bad, so he made sure we couldn't close the windows!! It was a really bad start to a really bad week without Ben.

It wasn't that I was trying to, but every day when Ben would call, I would end up crying on the phone. Not only was I behind in printing tax donation receipts, but the camper registrations were arriving and there were stacks of papers on my desk. One day was particularly difficult as my children seemed to be arguing and complaining more, and I tearfully told Ben that I, *"just couldn't do it anymore."*

Yet all along God was at work in two special ways. It started when some of our volunteer staff that had gone that weekend to Kansas City to have a booth for Camp David at a fair. It was a team of three alumni staff and their goal was to recruit staff, and find sponsors for campers. Nothing really interesting happened at the fair, but the team was pleased that one person had handed them a check for $50 for the camp. That day as I was returning from the airport and Ben was flying to California, the team unloaded from the trip at our house and one of them pulled out the check to leave it on my desk with a note. This time as she looked at the check that she had previously just glanced at, she realized that it wasn't for $50; the check was for $5,000!! I got a phone call instead of just a note that afternoon!! When I called Ben that evening to tell him the exciting news, we discussed how this money could help us build another camper cabin.

The second way God was working was in opening Ben's eyes to the real need at that time, and He used the conference to do that. While in San Diego, Ben sat through several workshops and took notes. One particular workshop was on burnout and how families must come before ministry. They also challenged husbands to really watch out for burn-out in their wives. It wasn't hard for Ben to realize that I was experiencing burn-out. It hit Ben that my need for help in the office was really the most important issue for the camp to address. Instead of building another camper cabin with that $5,000 (which God did provide the funds for in another way), God was leading Ben to use the $5,000 as His provision to hire a secretary for camp. The camp had never hired any staff before. Everyone volunteered (this was before Linda, our Horse Program Director, joined the team full-time). But it was time for change.

Ben got a phone call the next day concerning a young lady that had applied as a summer camp counselor, and in conversation Ben realized that this gal had recently left a secretary-type position at another company, and then it clicked in his mind—she could become our first hired secretary!

Not only did hiring a secretary help with all the paperwork, but I felt that God really had heard my cries and had provided for me. I could feel His love for me, and that was so comforting. I knew I could go on from that point.

᠁

There are times when our campers feel like giving up too. Each of us can be part of helping them to keep hanging on instead of giving up. My sister, Susie, wrote this about not giving up after serving as a counselor one summer. I think it's a wonderful reminder.

"I have been working at Camp David this summer... I have learned so much the last two months... I have been able to hold hands and pray with a dear little girl, her first prayer, asking Jesus to come into her life. I have been able to help a child dry her tears because she realized someone in this world loved her. I have been able to kiss the precious hand of a little girl who has never known her daddy. I have been able to be the big sister to a little boy who said his real sister was in prison and he has not seen her in three years. I have been able to worship and dance with a little girl that had no idea what it was like to see the sunrise. I have been able to dress up as a princess with a little girl who never in her life had put a dress on to look pretty. I was able to pick daisies with a nine-year-old that has never before in her life picked flowers. I have never felt so ... complete before. It makes me feel so small knowing that I have these little ones that are looking up to me, but then at the same time, I have never been happier with my work. It is hard, very hard at times... but God is so faithful. There was one evening my little campers were very tired and not listening to what I was telling them. I was emotionally and physical drained of energy. I just wanted a break from all of the fussing and clingy hands. I knew that I could not go on ... I needed strength...so I cried out to God and said, "Please just hold my hand and pull me along as I reach behind and pull my campers along with me. Give me strength Jesus, I need you to just give me your awesome grace to go on even when it's hard." It was wonderful... immediately it

felt like a huge load was taken off my shoulders... I suddenly wanted to sing... and show the campers that life is good... **and that we should never, ever, give up.**"

Never give up on loving.

Chapter 31

A Baby Born during Camp

There are two things in my life that have really brought me closer to God— having to trust God to provide for the needs of the ministry, and having babies. God brought both of these stretching experiences together with my fifth baby. After I had gone through such a difficult pregnancy and birth with our daughter Katy, I told Ben I really didn't want to ever have to go through that again. Not that I didn't want more children, but I didn't want to be pregnant again. At that time, our oldest daughters began to ask if we could adopt, and after a bit of discussion Ben and I thought we would start on the path to adopt some African-American babies. I even purchased some books on transracial adoptions and studied up on the subject. I also got the paperwork for us to fill out to apply to be foster parents to adopt. In talking with a local foster mom, I learned that black boys are the hardest to find adoptive homes for. When I shared that with Ben and our older children, our hearts were stirred with compassion for those boys. But several months later, the fostering papers were still in my nightstand next to my bed because Ben didn't have peace about filling them out yet. He felt we needed to wait. That fall, I started to feel nauseous close to mealtimes and having headaches—a typical sign I was pregnant. I was scared, big time.

A pregnancy test confirmed that I was pregnant. WHAT!! Didn't God know that meant my baby would be born DURING CAMP?? How crazy was that! But it was true. I knew it was important that my baby didn't feel rejection in the womb, and I wasn't trying to reject my baby. I was overwhelmed with the thought of going through another bad pregnancy and birth, AND of having a baby during the already extremely busy and stressful camp season.

Our other children were all thrilled with the news of another sibling, and our extended families were all excited for us too. I felt like I was the only one struggling with the idea. Then God gave me a verse that I held onto that entire pregnancy, "*Every good gift and every perfect gift is from above, and comes down from the Father of lights...*" (James 1:17) I was reminded that our new baby was a gift, and my Father God gives *good* gifts to His children.

One night Ben and I discussed all that had happened from hoping to adopt an African-American baby to finding out we were unexpectedly pregnant again. Suddenly Ben had a twinkle in his eye. "What if we named the baby an African-American name?" Instantly I loved the idea. It was something totally out of our norm. Our other kids all had very traditional or Biblical names. So we began writing down names of our campers that we liked, and I even ordered an African-American baby name book from Amazon. In light of the fact that we were having an African theme at camp that summer, it seemed to really fit to pick an unusual name for our baby that would be born during the year of our African Adventure.

I also began making plans to hand over my responsibilities to someone else so I could take a "maternity leave" for summer camp 2010. The first person I thought of was my cousin Leah, who lived in Florida. I knew she had been in camping ministry for years, she was organized, and as a single school teacher she would have her summer off. Leah prayed about it and agreed to join our team that summer! I tried to come up with lists of what I did, and explain all the different things she would need to manage in my place. There were some things I realized that we had different skills in, so I knew there would be a few things I'd have to do but I kept trying to tell myself and our team that I was going to be taking off "work" that summer.

As camp began, one night stood out to me. I had prayed so hard that my baby would be born early, so even though it was still a week before my due date, I was looking for any indication labor was starting. That evening I had a little sign that could be taken as impending labor and my pulse raced.

Then I heard the news. The weather monitor was going off and we were under a tornado warning! The problem was that our "tornado shelter" was the basement of our new building project and there were not steps into that building yet! And it's a fact that it's not easy for a big pregnant woman to climb into a building. But now with the storm heading our way, I had to go inside it for safety. I was scared as I stood beside the plank that was leaned from the ground up to the doorway, and watched everyone else easily walking up the plank to get to safety. With the "watermelon" that I was carrying in front of me, I felt sure I was going to lose my balance and fall, and then Ben showed up and was so sweet and helped steady me as I gingerly walked up the plank. Once in the basement I was safe, but then I began worrying that maybe I would go into labor down there with all that excitement going on. (People around me were pretty scared of the storm!) Singing hymns together helped bring peace to my heart, and thankfully the storm passed without any harm. My baby also decided to wait another two weeks to make his appearance!

I went into labor the night of the Princess Dinner. I felt fine during the special dress-up event, but that night my contractions started again. By 4 am, I woke Ben up and we began walking up the camp driveway and down the county road. Labor was slow, so after resting, we went for another walk around 6 am. At that time of the morning, our kitchen crew were arriving, and staff were stirring all over camp, and

I began to feel very awkward being in labor and taking walks. Thankfully, some dear friends in town offered to let us come to their house, so we said goodbye to our kids and headed for town. We alerted the Leadership Team that we were leaving, and it was an amazing feeling knowing that they were capable of handling things at camp, and we could actually leave. My friend Nikki took me for a long walk around the park in town, but by then my labor had really slowed. We tried several things to get labor going again (she was a physical therapist), and suddenly labor kicked back in and within 30 minutes Ben was rushing me to the hospital. Unlike my other four births, I had planned to have this baby in the hospital, with Nikki as my Doula.

Six hours later, we gave birth to a healthy baby boy, whom we named Jabari Benjamin. Jabari is Swahili (it rhymes with Safari), and means, "Valiant Warrior, Bringer of Consolation." That was a pretty heavy name with promise. All night and the next morning I told the hospital nurses, *"I have to get back to camp. I want the campers to be able to meet my baby before they leave to go home!"* Our Leadership Team had told us on the phone how the campers were all praying for us and the baby. But it was 10:30 am before I had signed all the paperwork so I could go home, and the campers had already left camp before I got there. However, our staff were still all there, and what a celebration it was!! Not only had they gone the extra mile and cleaned up my house while I was gone, but they had all signed a baby blanket for our new son (the campers had signed it too before they left!) I didn't need a thing. The team took care of my every wish and my baby was awed over by everyone. I felt like a spoiled mama, until Monday morning came.

15 hours after Jabari was born, we were back at camp, celebrating!

My mother has given me an incredible gift with each of my births. She comes to stay with me for about a week after I've had a baby and takes care of me and the rest of my family. Even though baby number five was born during camp, mom insisted on coming to take care of me. She arrived Monday morning to begin her week of caring for me and my newborn, but the staff all arrived then too. The camp office was still in my home, and Monday mornings are always crazy with trying to make sure the campers were at their pick-up spots and the drivers for all the routes knew who they were picking up. I remember standing in the doorway to the office, with my mom standing across from me. She wanted me to go lay down, but the staff had what seemed like a hundred questions for me. The reality that camp was not at a place for me to have a "maternity leave" hit me full force, and my shoulders sagged. My cousin was doing all she could down in Ft. Turley to take care of things there, but I still had to answer all the other questions in the office. I was able to finally sit down, but looking back, I realized that it did affect me. It took me almost twice as long as usual to recover from that birth. I really don't know what I could have done differently, but I am so grateful for my cousin being there, and everyone else that pulled a heavier load, so I could have a lighter load than normal. It was wonderful to have my mom there that week, as she did her best to "protect" me from working too hard (she was constantly reminding me to REST). One benefit to having a baby during camp season was that I didn't need to cook for seven weeks! One of my friends, Elizabeth, who was on our team, gave me a sling for my new baby. I began using the sling every time I walked around at camp, and I grew to love it. My baby could sleep in it, and I could keep him close to my heart all the time.

I was asked an amusing question from one camper as he looked at my little sleeping white baby: *"Is that thing for REAL?!!"* I loved telling the campers my baby's name and seeing them smile. Not many white babies are named Jabari. I was even told by one lady at a church, *"That baby's skin is too white for that name!"* I just smiled.

As I look back, I realize that God had me face some pretty big fears with sending us Jabari during camp. The pregnancy was actually a little better than Katy's pregnancy. The delivery and birth were very hard, but not as hard as Katy's birth, which was what I had been afraid of. And even though I didn't rest and recover as I wish I could have, I did make it, and it was really special having a newborn at camp that summer. My baby born during camp was a *good* gift.

Chapter 32

Still in Love

Ben and I made a presentation for Camp David in a local church service, and afterwards were in the foyer talking with different people about camp. When I finished one conversation I walked over to where Ben was and overheard him say, "*I sleep with the Assistant Director, so I should know!*" To this day I have no idea what the question was, but I did blush in that church foyer. Yes, when you put it that way, I do sleep with the Camp Director. And I'm his wife.

I'm so thankful that Ben and I share a dream. I've read that having a shared dream can really help a couple to have a stronger marriage, and I agree. It gives us a common goal, something to work on together. I love the times when the creative juices are flowing and we both get excited while brainstorming and planning together! It is so energizing!

When I hear other couples talk about their lives, I realize what a gift it is to be able to work side-by-side with my husband. We don't have HIPAA laws that make it impossible to share with each other about those we have contact with. Ben and I don't work odd shifts; we have the privilege of making our schedule together and sharing our parenting together. When I have a deadline to meet with a design project, Ben will often offer to make supper. When he is working late painting a camp room to be ready for a rental group, I often go down and help him paint. We actually enjoy being together!

I am submitting to you now, though, having a shared dream or ministry can almost ruin a marriage because the ministry can take over every part of your life. For us, there are times when the ministry feels life-giving, but other times it feels life-sucking. Some days we are on cloud nine—like when we see God provide in a miraculous way or learn that a life was transformed through our ministry. We feel alive and fulfilled! Another day can look a little more like this: we get a critical email from a former staff person, our lunch is interrupted with a phone call from our camp cook who ran out of propane, and our overdue date night is delayed because someone showed up unannounced for a tour of camp. After days like this we feel drained and frustrated by the ministry. The key to keeping ministry from ruining your marriage is keeping these things in balance.

When you are married to your co-worker, it is easy to wake up talking about camp, to talk about camp while we eat, while we brush our teeth, and after we get in bed and turn the light out. One morning I was fixing my hair and talking about camp, while Ben was sitting in his chair doing his morning devotions. Suddenly he said, *"Grace, we have to stop this! Please do not talk to me about camp until after 8:00 am! That's when I'm 'at' work!"* Setting a boundary between work and our personal lives helped to preserve our sanity and to have a relationship beyond "Director" and "Assistant Director."

I am very blessed to have a husband who values keeping our love alive by setting aside time for date nights. We can't often afford to go to nice restaurants, but we can enjoy fast food together— without the kids! During the busy season our date nights often include a trip to Lowes' to pick up building supplies, but we can hold hands as we walk through the store! Our weekends away as a couple are usually built around attending a camp conference, or having a booth at a fair, but the travel time gives us a lot of talk time. Our biggest struggle is not talking about camp the entire time we are out! We have to really put effort into talking about other things—anything other than the MINISTRY. A few times I have even put a pack of cards in my purse and pulled them out at a restaurant. These unique cards have different questions on them that help people talk about their feelings and likes/dislikes. It seems tacky to have question cards sitting on the table at a restaurant, but sometimes we are so wrapped up in ministry that if it weren't for those cards, we'd never begin to start talking how we are feeling and communicate on a deeper level.

I am including this next story because I desire to be real with my readers. I want others to know they don't have to have it all together in order to serve God. Our marriage has had its struggles, and it is only God's grace that we are **still in love**.

Even though we were working on setting boundaries and making time to connect as a couple there were still things in our personal lives that were pulling us down. Those things from our past were continuing to break trust in our relationship and set us on a pattern of hurt and pain that after many years had grown into a very big mountain between us.

We had been to counseling, which helped some, but in time the struggles would resurface and the wounds would be reopened. I finally came to a place where I didn't know how I could keep going on. Then one of Ben's guy friends recommended that we go for marriage counseling at a place called *National Institute for Marriage*. The cost for their four-day "Marriage Intensive" was totally out of our ability, but in a short time several generous friends offered to give toward the cost. We also qualified for a partial sponsorship, but it still cost us a lot of money. In light of the struggles we were having though, we felt we had no other choice. If we couldn't make our marriage work, we would lose our family, and we would lose the ministry.

It was a cold January day in 2012, when we arrived at the National Institute for Marriage. As we walked into the beautiful facility, I kept my head down—I felt full of shame. We were in full-time ministry, but by participating in the marriage intensive, we were saying to others that we were having problems in our marriage. I felt like a failure. I listened carefully when the other couples introduced themselves, and I was surprised to realize that we were not the only ministry couple enrolled. Some of the other couples were in full-time ministry, and some of them were business owners. It struck me that we were all in leadership positions, and we were all there because we needed help.

My experience there rocked my world. With all the Biblical principles that I had been raised with and learned through church and books, I had never experienced anything like the marriage intensive. The first big concept that stood out to me was what we should NOT focus on when I communicate:

- Who is right, and who is wrong?
- Who is at fault?
- What really happened?
- What needs to be done?

I realized that I had spent most of my life in communication with others focusing on these things. I was always trying to figure out who was right, or what was right, and judging the other person by whatever standard I was holding up.

The next concept we learned about was the *Fear Dance*. I discovered that Ben really desires acceptance, but he often feels judged by me, and he reacts to feeling judged by either defending himself (which makes me feel like he doesn't care) or by withdrawing and shutting down emotionally. Once Ben and I saw our fear dance mapped out, we were excited to learn how to care for our hearts and stop the fear dance!

The most significant concepts I experienced from the marriage intensive were grace and value. Grace to not have it all together. Grace to see things differently. Grace to step away and take time to care for my heart. Understanding my value in God's eyes was even harder for me to grasp. Even though I am a woman, God values *me*. I am not inferior, or helpless—God sees me as valuable and important in His kingdom. As I grasped my value, I was able to see how valuable my husband was and my love for him grew.

That week God began healing our hearts, and helping us to empathize with and understand each other. While we drove home from the marriage intensive, we excitedly discussed how the principles we were learning could really impact the lives of the campers and our entire camp community! We couldn't wait to see what God was going to do the next summer.

That summer at camp, Ben taught our campers and staff members about fear dances and caring for your heart. Several very difficult conflicts arose with staff that were able to be resolved by mapping out these two important concepts. Ben also used the new concepts to help resolve many conflicts with campers. It was thrilling to see relationships being healed and restored.

It has been over a year since the marriage intensive. Some of the old habits came back and created more pain, but we are making progress. We began meeting weekly with two other couples and working through the book, *The DNA of Relationships for Couples*, and realized that we have a long way to go to really learn to use the tools we've been given. It's simple things that make a difference like not judging our spouse before we hear what's on their heart, or softening our tone of voice so our spouse really feels cared for.

I no longer feel shame that we had to get help even though we were "in ministry." Admitting we needed help was the best decision we've made for our marriage. And we are in love more now than we were before!

Still in love, even during camp.

Chapter 33

Extending Grace

Sometimes people make comments about what a neat ministry we have started. It is only by God's grace that we have done anything. I am a perfectionist, and not always the easiest person for people to work with. Some days I get really uptight with wanting things to be just right, and people get hurt unintentionally. Other times Ben catches my eye and says, 'Grace, it's OK. It's all going to turn out great!" Relief washes over me as I remember, I don't have to have it all together! To me, the phrase "extending grace" is like the word "Despite." *Despite* me being irritable, my friend still smiles and offers to lend me a hand. *Despite* my husband forgetting about a family event, I choose to remember that he does care and give him grace. *Despite* worrying and trying to solve things ourselves, our Father God keeps providing for us.

I want to share Ben's heart about extending grace...
The word grace means a lot to me; maybe that's because Grace was the name of my middle school sweetheart, who is now my wife; maybe it's because of the grace my wife and others have

shown me at times when I was down or struggling. Extending grace to someone can have a significant impact, much like a long gentle rain after a two month drought. Grace is one of the most impactful parts of a new camper's experience at Camp David.

As children of prisoners, they start life with staggering liabilities, yet somehow society expects them to tow the line just the same. When they struggle, society answers, "You have to try harder!" At camp, these children experience something different. To help you understand their struggles, let me tell you a story about a boy we'll call Damion. While this Damion is a fictitious character, his struggles are real parts of our campers' lives.

On the bus ride to camp, Damion is leaning against the window watching cars go by and thinking... "Man, I'm hungry. We didn't have anything in the house to eat this morning. I hope the food at camp is good... Mom's boyfriend better not beat her while I'm gone... I wish my brother Lamont didn't get sent to prison. If only I had done what he told me to, but at least he gets to see our dad there... I wonder where my bag is, I hope they don't lose my clothes, they're all I have. Last time we were evicted Mom mistook my bag of clothes for a trash bag... I don't even have a sleeping bag. I told Mom that's why I couldn't go to camp but she asked them and the lady said they have sleeping bags there... oh shoot, what if I wet the bed! Man, I always wet the

SHAME is NO LONGER my name/ 213

bed when I am at a new place... I hate myself... I wonder what the paper said we would get to do at camp. I wish I could read the paper 'cause I think Mom probably lied about the camp...I hope they don't ask me to read..."

When Damion arrives at camp there is a snack waiting for him, and at each meal he can eat all he wants. When he gets to his cabin he is given a backpack with most of the stuff he will need at camp—like a tooth brush and toothpaste, a Bible, flashlight, and even a stuffed animal. The staff loan him a camp sleeping bag, and if he needs anything else they get it for him too—even things like a swimsuit or sneakers. When they go to bed each night, they pray for things he is worried about back home. For the first time Damion feels safe enough to talk about his dad's and brother's incarceration with others. When he wakes up with a wet bed, his counselor just quietly sends him off to the shower, and when he returns to his cabin later, he finds his clothes—smelling clean and neatly folded on a dry sleeping bag. When he struggles to read during devotions, his counselor notices and reads out loud for him. When he gets into a fight with another camper, a Counselor Coach helps him work it out, and the two boys become friends.

When Damion hears how Jesus extended grace to him by dying for his sins on a cross, Damion gets it! He has been extended grace, and experienced unconditional love all week long, and he knows it is true.

Lying in the dust at the feet of Jesus after being caught by a crowd in the very act of adultery, her shame must have been suffocating, death almost a sweet end. Jesus responds in the true character of the heart of God our Father, *"Let him who is without sin throw the first stone."* While He stoops and writes in the sand, her executioners, convicted by their own sin and shame, drop their stones and walk away. Oh, how I wish they had stayed because what He says next is for all mankind. When Jesus stood up, He saw no one but the woman so He said, *"Madam, where are your accusers? Hasn't anyone condemned you?"* And she replied, *"No one, Lord."* This is the part I wish they could have heard. Jesus says, *"Neither do I condemn you: go, and sin no more."* We have all failed God, we have all done wrong. The adulteress had done absolutely nothing to deserve this response. Yet Jesus, with no conditions says, *"I don't condemn you."* Releasing her from condemnation, judgment, and shame He paints a vision for her future. *"Go and sin no more."* That is what Jesus says to all of us, and He can because He paid the penalty for our sins on the cross.

This is the essence of Camp David. Showing our campers grace—and from that place of grace, inviting them to show that grace to others. Following is a story from Ben of two campers who had their eyes opened to the other's pain, which enabled them to share grace with each other.

While we welcomed the campers Monday afternoon, I could see Macy slouching in her chair, with her short cropped hair. It was clear that Macy was unsure about the whole camp thing. But before long she was enjoying cookies and milk with her team as they sat around the table and got to know each other. Macy came with her friend because it seemed like a nice escape from the drama of living with her mother, brother, sister and sister's baby back home.

On the second day of camp, over lunch, I heard someone angrily respond, "I am not afraid of you. If you wanna fight—we can do it right here!" Macy and her cabin mate Tyisha were standing and ready to fight. We quickly separated them and then showed them grace by listening to their frustrations. We sat with both of them together as they shared their feelings, helping each to empathize with the other. It was neat to see a change come over them. Sensing their new openness to each other, I ventured further with a question, "Would the two of you be willing to share your life stories with each other?" Over the next almost ten minutes, Macy and Tyisha shared stories of their fathers' incarceration, foster care, extreme abuse, rejection, and pain. In the end, they had a new compassion toward each other.

The grace Macy was shown at camp opened her heart to God as well. Macy put her faith in Jesus to forgive her of her sins and followed him in baptism. This winter I made a special trip to see Macy and her family. Macy greeted me with a big smile and hug when I arrived at their small home. I was excited to hear about her involvement in a local church and to see her desire to grow in her walk with Christ.

Playing with campers is just as important as helping them work through conflicts!

Chapter 34

The Ride Back

I have heard some stories about the bus rides back to St. Louis. Every once in a while the campers just fall asleep on the way home, but usually going home stirs up some really sad or mad emotions. It seems like it starts Thursday night with the walls going back up when the campers start thinking of going home the next day. Whatever they are returning to, they have to protect their hearts, and the happy little kids we saw Thursday morning have disappeared into either sad or mad campers by the time they are loading onto the buses. While we send them home with photo albums of their happy memories at camp, there are just a lot of emotions with the thought of them leaving and going home. Tears and hugs are common, as are bad attitudes—usually a cover up for emotions the kids don't know how to deal with.

I love how God uses every part of camp to impact these kids. From the good food to the hammocks hanging in our cedar trees each part is important. (Hammocks provide a rocking motion that kids who haven't been rocked as babies need.)

The bus ride home provides just one last chance to say to these kids, "There is hope! You can dream big for your life!" Our staff have written down two of their stories about the bus rides back home.

This story was shared by Kayla Norton, who has served several years as a counselor, and on our Leadership Team…

"The girls loaded onto the busses. I was the leader of the St. Louis bus route and head counting, bus rule reading and seat assigning is always a chore when you have a bus and van full of girls. Girls who are either excited to be going home or don't want to leave.

Somehow in the mess of loading, two young ladies got into the same van that weren't supposed to be together. Not 15 minutes from the camp, I called to check on the van and sure enough, there had already been a yelling fight. I instructed both drivers to pull over, and I took those girls onto my bus and sat the one who started it next to me in the front of the bus.

She was mad at me for moving her from the other van. She wanted to sit in the back of the bus by the other girls. As she threw her fit and yelled at me, I just took it and when she stopped to breathe I started to ask her questions and tell her stories about my past. "Why would a young lady want to act like this?" I thought to myself as I waited on her to reply to one of my questions.

I was surprised to see the changes in her face and the way she spoke. I talked to her not as the young child she acted like, but the adult she will someday be. She told me about her dream, where she lives, and how she hates school and her teachers. She also talked about the college she wants to go to and her dream job. But something that surprised me is how she had no knowledge of the world, other life styles and what was out there. She had no idea of what she could do with her life or how many choices she had. She only knew of her part of the city. When she asked me about my life, the look on her face was priceless. She's a city girl who rides skateboards and lives in a second floor apartment and I'm a cowgirl who lives on a farm, milks cows and rides horses.

That two-hour ride to St. Louis was the fastest trip I had that summer. She and I talked the whole way. As we pulled into the bus drop off, I watched her change from a witty young lady ready to take on the world, back into that unruly child again that I had sit next to me in the beginning of the bus ride. I don't know why she changed back like that, but it was almost like a light switch and took me by surprise. It made me wonder what she had seen in her past, or what she's going home to. But all I know is my heart sank into my stomach as I watched it happen.

Every week I've worked at camp, I've had a chance to see this or something much like it in the faces of campers. And every week I've wondered the same things as I did that day as I waved good bye. *Will I ever see her again? What will she be like the next time I do see her?"*

The next story is from MaKayla Cook, who is a published young author. MaKayla flew from Texas to serve at camp two weeks. Her story also touches my heart...

"The junior boys completely blew me away with their curiosity for God, their willingness to learn about Him, and their overall ability to create close bonds with their wagon teams. As one of the photographers for that week, I had made several friends among the boys, and enjoyed getting to know each of them better.

One such young man, whose name was Joey, captivated my curiosity especially. He could be so sweet, and try so hard one second, and then be tearing down a fellow teammate, or pushing the limits the next. I could physically see some of the insecurities Joey faced, but there was little to do in changing them, over the course of one week. So I took time to try to find moments to encourage him in things he could succeed at, and at times when he chose to do the admirable thing. Still, I wanted to know more about this young man, yet knew I had to wait on God (and Joey) to give me those answers.

Finally, on the bus ride back to St. Louis, God began to work between Joey and me. First, it started with a lot of filthy cuss words and jokes on Joey's part (leading to what I thought would be the most miserable two-and-a-half hours of my life), and I, nonchalantly asking him the purpose behind saying them. Was I missing something funny? This threw Joey off a bit, and began to make him upset that I could call him out in such a discreet way. He then began to sort of taunt me, saying, "I bet you never had a bad life. I bet you never had anything bad happen to you. You don't know what it's like!"

I sat there for a few moments, waiting for a bit of the awkward silence to sink in, just watching him. Then I began in a hushed tone, so he would have to tune in to me among the noise of the bus, "Do you know my story, Joey?... Do you know where I come from?"

"Well, no!" he sort of burst, "but it can't be that bad!" I went on to share with Joey my life story of hurt, betrayal, mistakes, adoption, acceptance of Christ, and fight against a life and devil that wants me to fail. By the end of my story, Joey, and most of the other junior boys on that bus, were quiet, and tuning into the two life stories being shared at the back of the bus. Soon other boys began to jump into our conversation, with stories about trials in their life, how they had overcome them, and what they were going home to. I leaned over to Joey and said, "If it were my guess, you and I aren't the only hurting people on

this bus.... we're not the only ones who have felt alone and unwanted at times... and we're definitely not the only fighters." We went on to discuss ways to fight the 'system,' how to dream big, and be different than who we are sometimes expected to be. As the bus rolled into St. Louis, and our destination neared, tears were streaming down the face of a young man whose eyes had been opened for the first time to the reality of other peoples' pains and fears, and the awesomeness of a God who still loves them through it all, and who will never leave them, like so many others have. The tears of one of the biggest camp bullies, quickly sobered the rest of the boys, and they, too, witnessed the power of God's peace in a young person's life, who had so much unrest before his eyes were opened. God used my life and words to witness to a young man who had lost hope in ever being loved."

Chapter 35

Giving Hope

The vision God gave us when we started Camp David has grown. But at the heart of everything is the desire to GIVE HOPE. As we bestow value on prisoners' kids and help them see their own worth, it gives them hope they can succeed. When we extend grace to them while they don't "have it all together," we are giving them hope. When we reveal the Father to them, and they realize they are loveable— they are filled with hope. When they hear the best news in the world— that Jesus has offered them new life through His gift of salvation, they have TRUE HOPE.

One of the ways God lead us to give hope in our camp program was by providing, "Stories of Hope."

Growing up, my parents would put the radio on each Sunday afternoon and we would listen to another episode of "Unshackled," by Pacific Garden mission. Most of the real life stories that were featured on that program were of people that had come to a point in their lives when they were completely without hope, and then they turned to God and their lives were transformed. Week after week of hearing stories of people overcoming addictions and hearing God's voice, really strengthened my faith as a young Christian.

When we started camp, both Ben and I knew that having people come give their testimony to inspire our campers was a key factor to giving them hope. So for many summers we had a coordinator (Ben's dad!) who would contact people and ask them to come out to camp during our evening chapel meeting and give a ten minute testimony. We knew it had to be short enough to keep the campers' attention, but long enough to tell a story that they could connect with. Many people from local churches came out. Some were recovering addicts who came from lifestyles much like our campers. Others were successful businessmen and educators who had started life as underdogs but had turned to God and through his grace had succeeded in rising above their "statistics." If you could have heard the hush that would come over the room when someone on stage would begin telling their story—you would understand how important these stories were. Often when campers arrived at camp or would see me in the morning, they would stop me and ask, "*Mama Rose, is someone going to give their testimony tonight?*" And I would respond that yes, there would be someone there. Many kids have said it was their favorite part of camp.

As the years went by we realized that each of our staff and counselors had stories to tell—maybe not with overcoming addictions, but most people struggle at some point in their lives to forgive someone that has hurt them. Many people know what it's like to feel rejection, or to be bullied, or to be filled with fear. When those staff people become real about their personal struggles on stage, and tell the campers how God helped them overcome them, it ignites a flame of hope in their hearts. They realize that God can do the same for them.

This precious young lady has a story of finding hope in Jesus at camp.

Later, in the cabins, the campers have the opportunity to share their stories with each other. This puts hope in their hearts as they realize they are not alone. There are other kids out there struggling in the same way.

The truth is, we all have a story. None of us has arrived. Our journeys have all kinds of twists and turns. Some have a lot of flowers along their journeys, others have long stretches of barren land and huge mountains to climb. I've heard panic in the voice of more than one counselor when they learned they would need to write out a testimony that they could share at camp. I think often the panic came from feeling that only people who "have it all together" should give their testimony, and since they hadn't "arrived" at some spiritual mountain peak, they didn't have anything to share. But Jesus used tax collectors, prostitutes, and children with just a few fish in their lunch sack. He loves to use us—broken and scarred—to impact others. Revelation 12:11 states, "*They triumphed over him by the blood of the Lamb and by the word of their testimony*..." Many times as staff have shared their testimony, God brought healing to their hearts through them retelling the story. Bringing those sad and painful things from the past to the light and seeing how God lead them on their journey can bring hope to the very ones who are sharing. Have you told your story to anyone lately?

Here is a story from one of our campers whose life was changed...

"When I was about 9 or 10 I found out my dad was going to prison. I had no idea what to think. I never really grew up in a Christian home. Then I found out about Camp David. I went and everyone was so nice. I had confidence issues, and I still do, but when I'm here at camp I feel loved and cared for. Before I

ever came here I felt worthless and stupid and that no one liked me, like I was a mistake. Then I learned my first year here that I am here for a reason. I looked forward to coming to camp every summer. Then when I finally turned 14 years old, I got to be Support Staff. I was looking forward to that the most! I was so happy when I got an invitation to do so. I could have gone to camp this year, but I decided to work there instead. I am so thankful that God has brought me here to meet all the wonderful people. He has taught me so much. When we sing in worship I can just feel his presence. This camp is so special to me. I learned my first year that God will always be on my side no matter what I do, and that he loves me and is there for me when no one else is. That when people ask where my father is or what he does, I can point up and say, "My Father is the Creator of the world and he loves me like no one else ever will."

Chapter 35

Developing Leaders

We had some very special visitors come to camp one day. Uddie, his girlfriend, and his brother Pete, whom we knew as "Petey". These visitors were special because they started coming to camp back in 2005! Ben and I met Uddie, Pete and their brother Billy (who was home sick), in December of 2004 when we were delivering Angel Tree Christmas gifts to their niece. Her father, their older brother, was in prison. The boys were ages 12, 10, and 8 at the time. That night, sitting on a dirt-covered floor, in front of their giant screened TV, Ben shared the Gospel story with them and they put their faith in Christ. We also invited the brothers to camp the next summer.

The three brothers came to camp for the next six years. Uddie would have only been able to come for one year, if we had not decided to start having senior camps in 2006 for ages 13-16. Some of the big things we did differently during our senior weeks was to teach life skills classes, like cooking and car mechanics. Then in 2007, we decided to add one more week of camp and make it a Leadership Training week. Our heart was to give our campers opportunities to grow spiritually and to develop a work ethic, which would open a lot of doors for them in life. Uddie was one of our first "Timothy Trainees," and we were able to cheer him on as he moved from just a camper to summer staff! Wearing an "orange" shirt is a real privilege at Camp David! Uddie's brother Billy followed in his footsteps and served on staff too. During the summer of 2008, while both brothers were serving on staff, Uddie wrote this testimony, "*I used to lie and steal a lot, but then I met Ben and Grace. They told my family about Camp David. Then my brothers and I went, and it changed me. I learned more about God. Then every year I came back and now I'm staff.*"

While former campers, Uddie & Petey, were visiting, we caught a glimpse of how much camp had impacted them.

I don't think I've ever had so much fun taking anyone on a tour of camp as I did when Uddie and Pete came to visit. Walking together around camp, the brother's mouths dropped open as they saw all the improvements and how nice Ft. Turley looked. As we visited each area of camp, they talked about their many happy memories, from the "*three-hour- long water battle with the Indians*" to the way Billy used to pull campers over the climbing wall! Uddie proudly pointed to one of the covered wagon cabins and said, "*Yeah, I helped build that wagon!*" That had been one of the projects he had worked on as a Timothy Trainee. Passing the basketball court, Pete said, "***These were the BEST childhood experiences EVER!***"

Uddie has graduated from high school now, and Billy was going to graduate just a few days from their visit. Pete is still in school. Ben and I are really proud of each of them. Ben asked Uddie what he is doing now. He said he is looking for a job and also running a lawn business that keeps his two brothers and his cousin all busy. They are so determined to work that they are pushing the mowers around from job to job, because their transportation is down. When asked how he learned to do yard work, Uddie's answer was quick and honest, "**I learned that when I worked on staff here at camp. It keeps food on the table for six of us, and pays the bills.**"

Camp had really made a difference for those three brothers. It provided their best childhood experiences and taught them leadership skills, work ethic, and how to care for lawns. With what they had learned and experienced, they were now supporting six people and paying their bills.

There is one more step beyond giving hope, which we realized is essential to breaking the cycle of crime in children of prisoners. It is giving children of prisoners the opportunity to **give hope to others**.

We believe that one of the greatest values CDO provides is the opportunity for everyone to discover the joy and excitement of helping others. There is something significant that happens when you stop thinking about yourself and focus on giving to another. I watched this unfold with wonder one morning. One of our campers, Cayleigh, had come to our Timothy Training week and graduated, which meant that we felt she was ready for the responsibility of joining our staff team. Cayleigh was so excited to be able to return to camp for three more weeks that summer— as Support Staff! Then came Wednesday, the day of the Princess Dinner. Cayleigh was assigned to help the young campers pick out their dresses to wear that evening. I was in and out of Fort Turley that morning, but every time I went in, Cayleigh would run up to me and give me a report on the dress finding. She was practically dancing as she told me, *"I helped Gabriel pick out a dress! I showed her ones I wore as a camper, and helped her find a black and red one that fit her perfectly!"* One camper, Angel, had been trying the patience of her counselors all week, and now she was refusing to make a decision on a dress. Cayleigh decided to make it her mission to connect with Angel and help her to find a dress. And she succeeded. Cayleigh talked about that the rest of the day. The opportunity to help other girls feel beautiful, as she had felt as a camper, was worth more than gold to that young lady.

Giving our campers the chance to develop leadership skills and serve as staff, directly combats the victim mentality that is common with children that have experienced abuse and neglect. We see this victim mentality each week of camp. It creates a sense of powerlessness in kids, and makes them feel like they are justified for breaking the rules. Their thinking goes something like this, *"If people aren't fair, the rules no longer apply to me,"* or *"If it's not my fault, it's not my responsibility to do something about it."* By offering campers the chance to take responsibility, work hard, feel the satisfaction of a job well done, and bring a smile to someone's face, we change their outlook on life. They realize *they* can be a solution to the problems around them. *They* have something to give. *They* can make a difference.

A few years ago, one of our board members, whose family served at camp, began to question the ministry focus of Camp David. He had heard so many staff talk about the impact serving America's most at-risk children had made on them, that he began to feel that maybe we should re-adjust our focus to see the potential in training leaders. This brought quite a debate, as some argued that we were a specialty camp for children of prisoners, and others focused on the life-changing impact that camp had in raising up young leaders.

After a lot of discussion and prayer, Ben and I, as founders, were asked what was the heartbeat of why *we* do camp. We both came to the same conclusion. It was the kids, and children of prisoners, especially. But right under that mission, was our desire to train leaders. The result of that debate was a revised Mission Statement that reflected our passion for developing leaders: **To be a transforming agent in the lives of children of prisoners by introducing them to the love and hope in Jesus Christ, and to develop leaders who will impact our world.**

In the safety of a caring community, young people take leadership roles, share their faith, and take responsibility for making camp the best it can be. Camp David **is** developing leaders.

Developing leaders who will impact our world.

Chapter 37

In My Laundry Room

Remember how I said I was excited when we got our mobile home moved to camp, because now there was an office at camp? It really was an incredible blessing to have the office and our home at camp, but as the years went by it became harder and harder to share the space, which was being filled with more and more people! As camp grew, so did the needs, so my home wasn't just the "office" during camp. I hosted meetings, overnight guests, had an open door policy for staff who needed showers, and it was a hang-out place.

Staff would show up sometimes around 5:30 am to take showers (because there weren't enough down at camp) and that would turn into a steady flow of traffic that would continue until up to 10 pm. Since Ben's and my bedroom is directly next to the office, it created some awkward moments for us. Like when we'd be getting ready for bed and suddenly hear a printer start, which meant a staff person had come into the office to print forms, again.

When we hired our first secretary, I had to adjust to a young lady showing up at my front door every morning during the school year. Our kids had to keep it a little quieter once the secretary got there at 8:30am. We tried to keep the front door area vacuumed and the microwave clean as the secretary would need it to warm up her lunch. At 4:30pm when she would head home, I would always relax a little more. While I did enjoy the company and our secretary and I became good friends, it was hard to focus on homeschooling when there was an employee working in my home. There were always questions to be answered. The next summer during camp, I felt I came to the end of my ability to extend hospitality as my home was again invaded by an army of staff.

During summer camp 2011, one day in particular stands out to me. In the office in my home two staff girls were working. There were also two staff girls at my dining room table making phone calls to campers' families. Later in the morning, a group came into my house for a class in the living room, which is open to the dining room. This meant the gals that were making phone calls had to find quieter places to call...like sitting in my kid's bedrooms. As the morning went on, I remembered that I was behind on laundry, so I headed back to my laundry room to change over loads. As I opened the laundry room door and stepped in, I was startled to find yet another staff person trying to make phone calls!! They were as startled as I was, and I sensed they felt bad for being there. In my head I understood that they were just trying to get their job done, but something inside me snapped at that point! I didn't have one place in my house that I could "retreat" to, not even my laundry room.

I called one of our new board members, who was also a mom of some of our staff and who had been a missionary in Africa for ten years. She told me I had to set boundaries. Living like this wasn't healthy, and I must ask staff to shorten their hours so I could at least have my early mornings and evenings free. When I told Ben about what had happened and what our board member said, he totally agreed. So we talked to all the staff, and they were very understanding and respectful of our need to have some "space." We also began to make definite plans to build an office building the next year.

What a joy it was the next spring as we broke ground on the new office building!! I had made most of the building plans, patterning off of another office building in town that I liked. The new building would have a conference room (no more classes in my living room!), a reception area with our secretary's desk so she could greet people, and four smaller offices on the sides of the building. Funds for the new office building were slow in coming, but we were very grateful for a generous donation of $15,000 that helped us get a good jumpstart on the project. It was a busy spring in our community, and when we would announce work days, we just had a few dedicated volunteers that were able to come out. Ben's dad and another one of our board members came almost every day for a few weeks. I knew they were doing it for our family because they didn't want us to have to host the office in our home again. Since our supply of skilled carpenters was low, our children learned to help set rafters with their dad. It was scary for me to see them up high working on the building, but they did great and were a huge help in getting that building framed in (and it was fun to work with dad!). We had broken ground on April 12, 2012, and by the end of May there was drywall on most of the walls, and we were ready to move in. The biggest inconvenience was that the bathroom wasn't up and working yet, so all summer everyone that worked in that building had to run to Fort Turley to "use it." But there was electric, internet and air conditioning, so we had what was really important! And best of all, my home became a "retreat" for our family— a quiet place we could escape to in the midst of a crazy summer.

Now as we prepare for our 10th year anniversary celebration, I can look at the carpeted, painted, and trimmed office (including a flush toilet!) and see another example of God's amazing care. A group from the United Methodist church had helped set the poles for the front porch, a Catholic university group hung the siding, a Baptist church group painted the siding, and a home church group hung the lights and put up trim. Members of the First Assembly of God hung the doors and did the plumbing, electric and HVAC. A service team from Michigan painted the trim, and the list goes on and on. Our administration building is an amazing example of the body of Christ working together to give hope to troubled kids.

Setting the rafters...

Our daughter, Bethany

Ben

Ben with his dad

Families from "My Father's World" company came to help right before camp!

The new administration building was built by so many caring families in our community, and groups across America

Chapter 38

Inside a Maximum Security Prison

After nine years of being in camping ministry, I felt the need to connect more with those in prison ministry, so with Ben's agreement, I signed us up to attend a conference in North Carolina for prison evangelists in 2012. We were the youngest attendees at the conference, but we were so blessed to learn from all those saints who were going inside heavily locked and guarded prisons and ministering to God's church that was inside the prisons. I heard a lot of testimonies of men who had been in prison for many years, and their life-changing encounters with God. While it was all very encouraging and I felt I was learning a lot, I didn't really connect with those men in prison until I went myself.

I am used to being around prisoners' children, and I hear some very heartbreaking stories of how their daddies abused them, or hurt their little hearts. I didn't realize it, but I had built a wall in my heart towards those dads that had hurt their little ones. They had sorta become big, mean monsters in my mind.

The COPE prison conference officially ended on Friday night, but we had signed up to be part of a team with Forgiven Ministries to host a *One Day With God* camp inside a maximum security prison. We had filled out extra paperwork before the conference so we could go into the prison, and we listened carefully to all the rules about what to wear and what to take (our driver's licenses), and what we would *not* be allowed to take into the prison.

Ben and I were pretty excited as we headed to the Forgiven Ministries facility. We were used to camp ministry in the rural Ozarks, but we knew we were in for something so different! They assigned us to be mentors to three children all from the same dad, but with different moms. I don't know why, but I was surprised as our mentees walked to us. They looked just like our campers! In a short time we were instructed to load onto the buses for a brief ride over to the prison. Only two of the three children had arrived, but they talked non-stop on the way to the prison. The thing they argued about the most was which one looked more like their dad. They also talked about the last time they had seen their dad, and what his favorite things were.

I had heard other people's stories about their first visit in a maximum security prison, and how when the doors shut, they felt trapped. But because my attention was on making our mentees feel safe, there wasn't time for me to feel scared.

When we got to the large gym, we had to wait for the leader to call the inmate's name, and then the child's name, before we could enter. As the inmate that was father of our mentees walked towards us, our kids ran to him. Instantly a big lump was in my throat. I walked into the room and watched from the side as dad after dad was called to the main door and then hugged his child for the first time, in a very long time. One of the little girls had never even met her dad before that day. Forgiven Ministries volunteers had driven for hours that morning to pick up some of the children whose mamas had really wanted them to be able to see their dads but could not bring them.

The dads who got to spend that one day with their kids had to earn the privilege to see them by their good behavior in the prison for months prior to that day. Research has shown that if they have one day with their child, they are much more motivated to continue their good behavior for months afterwards. It is also beneficial for the children to see the reality of where the cycle of crime takes people, which will hopefully help them to make different choices with their lives.

I was very impressed when I learned that the Forgiven Ministries Team had actually gone into that prison the day before and spent an entire day teaching these men how to be dads. They taught them how to bless their children, and even how to sing crazy camp songs so that when their children arrived on Saturday, they would know the songs!

The program officially started with an "inside field game" including orange cones, balls, and lots of running. I began to relax some as the games were familiar to me. It really felt like camp, inside a prison! From the craft time to silly songs, I watched dads that were covered with tattoos, in tan jump-suits, hugging and loving on their kids. And they became human to me— the big, mean monsters turned out to be dads who had made mistakes.

One thing that surprised me was that they celebrated the children' birthdays while we were there, which reminded me of Camp David! The previous day the dads had filled bags with gifts to give their children (from supplies Forgiven Ministries provided). You could see the joy in their faces as they handed their child a gift and said, "Happy Birthday!"

I think I had a lump in my throat that entire day. God was bringing me full circle. Long ago he helped me to empathize with prisoners' children that were struggling with shame, then he opened my eyes to the struggles prisoners' wives face, but now I was face to face with the prisoners themselves, known as "Dad" to their loved ones. My heart was filled with compassion for them as well.

Chapter 39

Doing it...together

Even before we got married, Ben and I were looking at joining a large mission organization as missionaries. Shortly after getting married we began finalizing our plans. As we began to fill out the paperwork from the packet we had received, a concern came up that we really couldn't ignore. We realized that if we were going to serve on this mission organization's base overseas, we would be required to put our children in their day cares and schools. They considered both husbands and wives to be employees in their organization, and families on their base were not allowed to homeschool. It was our heart to homeschool our children, and serve God together— as a family. With sad hearts, we laid aside the application and chose to trust God to guide us to the place he had for us—a place that would include our whole family.

Ben's grandparents were missionaries in Morocco back in the day when you were expected to leave your children in boarding schools in order to fully serve the Lord. We had heard first hand stories of the damage this had done to their children, and we didn't want our children to go through that kind of pain.

Over the past ten years, I have met a lot of families involved with Christian camping. Some families choose traditional schooling, and some of them homeschool. When we met Cliff and Susie Johnson, directors of the first camp for children of prisoners in Missouri, we were impressed with how they were serving God as a family. We watched as husband and wife worked side by side to lead the camp ministry. They homeschooled their children, and the children were part of the ministry from directing puppet skits to praying for the campers. In talking with their young people we could see they were excited to be part of the camp ministry. Now ten years later, we sadly had to say "Good-bye" to Cliff as he was diagnosed with lung cancer and went home to his Maker on April 17, 2013. At Cliff's funeral I listened carefully as his adult children shared about their dad. What impressed me was that those who had grown up as part of the camp ministry were now serving God with their husbands and children. Some were heading to the mission field overseas, others were involved with youth ministry, but they were all passionate about reaching others for Jesus Christ—just as their dad had been. Their family ministry had stood the test of time in my book, and had borne good fruit.

Our visit with the Johnsons ten years ago affirmed our desire to serve God together as a family. Now we have five children, including two teenagers and a toddler, and we are serving at camp together. I asked my kids what it is like to grow up as a C.K. (camp kid). I wanted them to talk about the good and the bad! At first they struggled to put into words what they felt about it. Finally my second born, Esther said, *"Well, it's fun! And it's hard when you get really busy* (meaning when her parents are busy), *and I get tired. But I like helping people and seeing kids from our community turn to God and the difference that makes in their lives."* Then my first born, Bethany, added, *"My Sunday School class was recently studying the beliefs of different church denominations. As they discussed one after another, I realized I've been in* that *church to speak about camp, and that* church, *and I know people from* that *church denomination that have come out to camp. It hit me that because of the camp ministry, I had a much bigger picture of the body of Christ than most of my classmates did; and to me that's pretty neat."* A few days later Esther was talking about one of her friends, who often feels like she stands out because her skin is chocolate and we live in a very vanilla community. Esther realized that she never really notices the difference in skin colors, and she said it was camp that had made that "normal" for her.

The stories my kids told, made my heart sing. I love that serving in an inter-denominational ministry to urban youth has torn down a lot of the walls that typically divide people. They can look past skin color and church signs and see the value in each person.

Sometimes my kids complain because of the work. During the off-season they have often been the ones to mow and weed whack, sweep and mop Ft. Turley, and clean the bathrooms for work teams and rental groups. On the other hand, just as I learned to work hard on my parent's farm growing up, my kids are developing a good work ethic and character by serving at camp.

This summer, volunteer camp grandparents commented to me that they were blessed to see our kids conversing easily with guests of all ages. After camp my Bethany commented, *"Mom, all of us kids are leaders. That's what camp does to us!"* Growing up as C.K's is helping them to become leaders and problem solvers, and to develop public relation skills. It has also provided them with opportunities to grow in areas they enjoy like creative writing, working with horses, or being on the camp worship team.

My son Timmy's favorite part of camp is meeting new people and making friends. He also likes to help people, and there are a lot of opportunities to do that! One day I was in town getting supplies for camp and my trip took longer than I expected. Suddenly, I realized that Ben had left camp for a meeting and my 10-year-old son Timmy was still there. I called the camp office to ask our Office Manager, Rachel, to check on my boy. I figured he could help our Facility Manager, Josiah, or walk up the hill to his grandma's house. Rachel called me back a few minutes later, "*I found Timmy. Our weekend work team has arrived and he was giving them a tour of camp!*" That's my boy. Someday he wants to be the camp director.

Katy likes meeting the campers, playing in the playhouse with the little girls, and dancing with the girls at the Princess dinners. She also loves being on the *Green Team*, a unique Day Camp program just for children of our

Katy playing with a camper

adult volunteers. Katy makes a lot of friends through that Day Camp Program! Jabari also loves running around on the Green Team. The campers think he is cute and are always giving him high fives and hugs.

While you may not be able to devote a whole summer to ministry, finding ways to serve God together as a family has lasting benefits. If you have never served together, I encourage you to give it a try! You could volunteer with a

Food Distribution Program and once a month hand out food to low income families in your community, or you could take a week long summer trip to help at a Navajo Reservation.

The Holmes family has volunteered at camp the past few summers. Dad Holmes is an engineer who takes off a week of work to serve as a "fix-it" guy around camp. Mom Holmes serves as a counselor. Their older daughters serve as counselors or help in the kitchen, and their youngest daughter is on the Green Team! There are many other family groups that come to serve too. It's fun to discover who is related to whom, and realize how many moms, brothers, sisters, and cousins are serving here together!

The biggest challenge in family ministry is setting boundaries (sounds familiar, right?). I've heard camp directors say they never see their kids during the summer, and I can see how that could happen. No matter where you serve God, you have to be intentional about protecting your family—physically, emotionally, and spiritually. Ben plans his evenings during summer camp so that he can come up to our house and tuck our little ones into bed. When he has to take a trip to town to pick up supplies, he will often take one of our kids with him to have some one-on-one time with them. We have made a lot of mistakes in not setting better boundaries, like when we allow weekend work teams to come for weeks in a row and we don't take any days off. After a while our kids start to make comments about how busy we are and we have to acknowledge their hurt and ask their forgiveness, rather than justify our actions. Creating an environment where they can talk about their feelings helps each one feel valued. To combat our workaholic tendency, we try to plan day trips just for the family (away from camp!) during the extra busy seasons.

One great advantage to living at camp is we get to eat most meals (during the off season) together as a family! We also do our best to guard our special Friday family nights. One family night as we sat at the table with the nice tablecloth on, the candles lit, and our best dishes on the table, Ben told the kids that no one was allowed to say one word about camp that night. If they did, they would have to kiss his deer mount in the den as their consequence!! Their eyes got big, and no one said anything about camp that night. Now the kids remind us of that rule on family nights!

The biggest blessing is the opportunity to watch God do miracles and to provide for all our needs. Our kids have seen their dad fasting and praying for God's provision. They have seen us praying together as a couple, and they know that God is the one we turn to when things are difficult. Two years ago, Ben read the biography of Lillian Trasher to us after our supper meals. It was an incredible story of a lady, full of faith and obedience to God, who crossed the ocean with just a few dollars in her pocket. She eventually started an orphanage in

Egypt that grew to over 600 children. We all sat on the edges
of our seats waiting to see how God would provide through
one crisis after another. Now my oldest daughter, Bethany,
wants to serve God in missions. I believe that our years of
stepping out in faith and trusting God for big stuff have played
a part in her desire to have her own adventure with God. My
second born, Esther, wants to go to beauty school and learn to
do hair and nails, and I know she will use those skills to help
girls see that they are beautiful and valuable. She will be
touching lives, too, and making a difference. I don't know
where my children's journeys will take them, but I know they
have experienced God's care and love in a very real way as we
have served together.

Our family Spring 2013
L-R: Katy, Esther, Grace,
Ben & Jabari, Bethany, and Timmy

Chapter 40

Something was missing

I love this story from Ben about Staff Training 2012...

"It was the last full day of Staff Training and I was wide awake at 4:00 am with the thought, "They don't really get it yet. Something is missing!" The staff had sat through classes, worked together on team initiatives, cleaned up camp, and played fun games, but I sensed that somehow we had missed the camp's significance for our campers. I did the only logical thing to do when you realize you're out of time and you missed the most important part of the annual training week: I prayed! "God show me what to do!" Before I got out of bed I had an answer. Among the 55 young people in training that week were four children of prisoners, two boys and two girls. Three were former campers. The idea was to create a "Panel of Prisoners' Children."

During breakfast I asked each of the four if they would be willing sit on a panel and answer a few questions, which I would give them beforehand. They all said, "Yes!" That night with great anticipation, I set up the stage with four chairs and a long table covered with a table cloth. After introducing the plan for the evening to all the staff, the four took their seats. I was a little apprehensive, with my greatest fear being that the experience would leave these four feeling more shame and guilt. I asked the first question, "How old were you when your parent was incarcerated?" Soon they were excitedly answering questions punctuated with tears, but also with laughter. The fear and shame of being a prisoner's child began to melt away. Hearing each others' stories caused each of them to want to share more of their own. Amongst the four there grew a deep sense of understanding. The sharing time ended an hour and a half later leaving the rest of our staff with tear-streaked faces and deep hearts of compassion for children of prisoners.

The first thing that stood out to me from the evening was the SILENCE that children of prisoners' face. Mom doesn't talk about dad's incarceration, grandma doesn't want to talk about it, and it is too risky with teachers and friends. There is no one in the long days and months and years after their parents' incarceration, to help them make sense of the thoughts that are racing through their heads. How significant it must be for campers to hear, during their first hour at camp, that they all have something in common—a parent in prison—and they realize it is safe to talk about it here!

The second thing that stood out to me was how many of them felt SHAME and REJECTION for their parent's incarceration.

Somehow they felt it was their fault or they were wrong. For some, this was coupled with a fear that they would turn out just like their parent that was behind bars. When asked, "What was the most helpful thing someone said to you regarding your parent's incarceration?" Three of the four couldn't think of anything, because NO ONE had talked about it. But one young lady remembered a school teacher telling her that she didn't have to become like her dad (a murderer). She could be anything she put her heart to be. She never forgot that. I am so grateful for the Camp David staff who affirm our campers each day, and I especially enjoy the last night of camp when we give each camper a certificate that acknowledges the good we see in their lives.

Another thing that stood out was how much they realized their need for God as young children. Two campers said they would pray to God several times a day. They really get that they need HIS help! Camp was the place where the ones that were former campers had learned how to talk to God, and where they learned about God's gift of eternal life.

I want to share just one more thing that stood out to me. The panel shared how while growing up they had no responsible adults to care for them. Several were cooking and caring for themselves and their younger siblings at seven and eight years of age. One had to raise her sibling who was a baby. One former camper said, "No one ever taught me how to sweep a floor. I *thought you swept the food under the table! At camp I learned how to sweep the floor and make my bed."* I am so grateful to all the staff who teach our campers how to wipe off tables, sweep floors, and say, "Please," and "Thank you."

The final words of one of the four went something like this, "You really need to try to understand these kids. There is a reason they are so bad. I was a really bad kid in school. I was mad at life. People would say, 'Why don't you just...' But they didn't get all that I was going through."

This is what Camp David is all about; extending GRACE, bestowing VALUE, giving HOPE and revealing the FATHER, to the least of these.

This is likely the first character award this camper ever recieved!

Chapter 41

Close down camp?

I believe! I believe in miracles because I've seen them with my own eyes. In the middle of summer camp 2012, we almost had to shut down camp. It was actually right before our biggest week of junior boys! The weeks prior to that we had been sending out our camp email updates and sharing that we really needed sponsors, but the camp funds were drying up fast. After five weeks of camp, on Monday July 9, my husband Ben told me that he wasn't sure how we were going to pay the food bill the next day when the U.S. Foods truck arrived. We began praying in earnest, and posted a prayer request for God's provision on Camp David's Facebook page. By the middle of the morning Tuesday we had enough funds to pay the food bill, but there were a number of bills that were due at the end of the week. We began fasting and spending extra time in prayer. You know the verse that says, "*Pray without ceasing*?" That's how our lives became—whether we were walking to the dining hall or to the new office building, we were continually in prayer.

On Thursday night, our Staff Ministries Director, Bruce, led the staff in a time of worship down by the campfire circle. I joined the team there, and with tears streaming down my face, I worshiped God with all my heart. I thought of many names of God such as "Wonderful Counselor, Mighty God..." and my heart was encouraged. While I gazed at the beautiful sunset overlooking the rolling Missouri hills, I asked God to increase my faith. A sense of peace came over me and I felt sure He was going to send a check in the mail the next day.

When our secretary arrived Friday morning I eagerly greeted her and asked what was in the mail. "Nothing but one more bill," she replied with concern. I was devastated. "God, is this your plan? To bring us to this point and now close down camp?" That afternoon at our staff debrief meeting Ben and I shared that unless a miracle happened, we would not be having camp the next week. We asked everyone to take home sponsor brochures and ask friends and family to sponsor campers. At that point we still needed 177 sponsors, and since the sponsorships help pay for summer camp, that is what we were praying for. As I went through the rest of that Friday, I felt quite numb. I pictured myself having to call all those moms as I do every weekend. Only this time instead of confirming that their children were coming to camp, I'd be telling them that, due to a lack of funds, we had canceled camp. I was sick to my stomach thinking about it.

Ben and I got up Saturday morning knowing we had to write a letter and send it to everyone on our email list. Our board of directors had told Ben it was time to let everyone know our situation. We wrote the email with heavy hearts. Down inside we wondered, "Had we done something wrong? Was this our fault somehow?" Now, months later, I firmly believe it was God's plan to show Himself strong— just like the Red Sea parting. We pushed the "Send" button for our email at 10:00 am, walked out of the office, and got into the camp van.

The fact that we had a camp van was a miracle in and of itself! We have been praying for several years for a van for the camp to help with transportation. Just the week before a generous family in our community donated a nice Ford conversion van to the camp!!

Now you are really going to think we were crazy, but we were getting in that van with our weekend staff so we could drive to some old mobile home parks in Rolla and invite kids to our Community Kid's Camp. Ben so believed that God was going to come through and provide the funds to keep camp open, that, in faith, we were out inviting more kids to camp while the miracle was happening online. All over America (and in Italy), friends of the camp were reading their emails and responding by donating online. At 10:12am the first notification of a donation made came to my inbox—3 campers were sponsored. By 11:04am, 5 more campers had been sponsored. By 2:00pm when we returned from our trip to Rolla, we opened our emails and were shocked to realize that 30 campers had been sponsored!!! We were going to be able to have camp the next week!!! As the donations kept coming in that afternoon, our whole family was in awe. My kids were watching a miracle right in front of their eyes! By Sunday night when our staff all returned for the junior boys' week, we were able to share with total amazement that God had provided $17,000 over the past 30 hours so that we could continue to have camp. The donations kept pouring in over the next two weeks. God is so good. And that's not the end of the story. In August, as we began matching sponsors and campers, we were delighted to find that ALL our campers had been sponsored for 2012!!! My heart was overflowing with gratitude to my Father God.

There was one more huge answer to prayer that happened after summer camp ended. For the previous five years we had been praying for another family to join our team. I listed it as a prayer request with each of our family newsletters, "*Pray for another family to join us in the ministry.*" At the end of August, Bruce and Michelle Cook responded to our invitation to join our team and said, "Yes!" to being our Staff Ministries Directors, year-round. The Cooks are parents to five kids, and have been ministering to youth for over 20 years. They also already had experience in camping ministry! Bruce is a trained adventure guy, so he does all our team-building initiatives with groups now! The Cook family is still raising missionary support to be full time with camp, and praying for God to provide housing. Also in August, Linda Collins (who had joined our team full time in 2011 as our Ministries Supervisor) got married!! Her new husband, Josiah Faber, had already been in camping ministry, and chose to join our team when they married! Now when we have once-a-week staff meetings, there are seven people—problem solving and praying together. What an amazing journey with God!

When you are faced with the possibility of having to close down something that you have worked so hard to create, you come face to face with why you are really doing it. The summer of 2012 was tough, but as tough as it was, we had also connected more with the campers and heard their stories more than ever before. Because we were working to create a safe place for campers to talk about the struggle of having a parent in prison, they opened up more than before. As we heard their stories and their pain, and it was at times almost more than our staff could handle. We had to give a few girl counselors time off just to work through the grief and heartbreak of hearing their campers' stories. One night Ben came home and wept from the heart wrenching stories he had heard. Another night it really hit me too- I was tucking my little girl, Katy, in bed and praying with her. Suddenly I realized that for some of our campers, camp was the only time during their life they got to listen to a bedtime story, and have an adult pray with them and tuck them into bed. I thought especially of three little boys that were at camp that week who lived in a hotel with their relatives. We had tried to reach their guardian that afternoon to ask permission for one of the boys to be baptized, and every adult in that hotel room was drunk or high on drugs. No one could give us an answer. I wept as I thought of those boys going to bed each night in an environment where their guardians were drunk or high.

There were several years when, as we came to the end of camp, I would ask Ben, "*Are you SURE you want to do this again?*" (I was always worn out and exhausted at that point.) Ben would always respond, "*Absolutely!*" After our ninth summer of camp, I didn't ask Ben that. I KNEW in my heart that the ministry was making an impact and God was taking care of us. I wanted to do it all over again, the next year.

Now, after ten summers of camp, we have served 1,253 campers total. Each summer we have about 150 volunteers, and some of those are former campers! As I read their camp evaluations at the end of each week of camp, I can tell you that camp is making a significant impact in both the campers and the volunteers.

Chapter 42

I Have a Dream

Do you have a dream? Have you heard God's whisper like we did? Have you tried to follow your dream, only to have things turn completely upside down? Maybe your dream feels like it is far away...like at the top of a mountain, and you have been walking around in a fog trying to find a path up the mountain. Maybe your dream seems so close you can almost feel it, but you can't grab hold.

As we prepare for Camp David's 10th year celebration, I am reflecting on all the aspects of the dream God gave us. It really started with a desire, even before we were married, to be part of something big that expanded God's kingdom. The box we had put that desire in was like a suitcase—with a tag for overseas missions. After getting married, we kept trying to charge forward, but there was a fog and we kept running into the mountain. At one moment in the year 2000, the fog lifted and we could see clearly that the path for us was going to require trading in that suitcase for a tent called camp. We tried to charge ahead again, but the fog drifted back down for the next two years, until God used a difficult time of sickness to help us focus and set our course straight. Now we've had that tent pitched for many years, and over time it was exchanged with a larger tent as camp has grown to more than *just* a summer camp program. What used to be our "off-season" is now filled with year-round mentoring, an after-school program, horse riding lessons, and hosting retreats and banquets. Ministry that is making a difference in God's kingdom is happening year-round.

I feel like I've hiked to a peak on this journey and the sky is clear so that I'm able look at the path I've come up. The path has wild flowers and large boulders at different points in the path. From this peak, I can also see the path ahead a short distance. There are more tents scattered in the path ahead, as our dream has grown. We can see mentoring programs to match moms and families together, attaining more land so the horse program can expand, and a HOPE Center started in East St. Louis as a refuge for children. We also want to help start new camps for children of prisoners across our nation. If we are really going to break the cycle of crime in America, we need camps for troubled kids outside of every major city.

Ben penned these words in May 2010. I was so inspired by them I made a movie with him sharing this that can be seen on YouTube (you may need a few Kleenex as you listen).

Would you picture with me Dr. Martin Luther King, Jr. standing on the steps of the Lincoln Memorial, delivering his famous speech? Now picture a much more rural setting, with our Camp Director Ben, behind the microphone...

"I have a dream. I have a dream of prisoners proudly showing pictures of their children's graduation, instead of a newspaper clipping of their son's mug shot and recent sentence.

I have a dream of our girl campers being presented as pure brides to young men who will love, cherish, and honor them, instead of being girls known for easy sex, whose babies never know the love of a father or worse, never see the light of day.

I have a dream of prisoners' children sharing the pain of their past in a setting where they are loved and cared for, rather than silently carrying their pain for the lonely remainder of their lives.

I have a dream of children of prisoners courageously taking on the pains of life with a certainty that God is good and He will work everything for good, rather than snuffing out all hope in a noose because their life didn't seem worth living.

I have a dream of sons of prisoners courageously defending the helpless with their own lives, rather than ending the life of a child in a drunken stupor.

I have a dream of our campers learning how to find comfort in safe relationships, rather than numbing their pain with drugs, alcohol, and sex.

I have a dream of an alumni camper raising his own children and laughing with them at the dinner table, instead of sitting helplessly in a lonely cell wondering if his ex-wife's boyfriend is abusing his kids.

The dream is still bigger...

I have a dream of the middle class teens being Christ's hands and feet bringing love and hope to broken children, instead of spending their youth pursuing the temporary joys of affluence.

I have a dream of adult children of prisoners serving side by side with the middle class young adults as counselors at camp and close friends, rather than looking at each other with contempt through the window of a car, wondering how someone could be so messed up.

I have a dream of an older widow getting a hug from a girl she just taught to sew, instead of sitting all afternoon watching the news and wondering what has become of the next generation.

I have a dream of mechanics and builders teaching sons of prisoners how to change oil and drive a nail, rather than hoping they stay away and hoping they don't steal their tools.

Each summer I see more and more of this dream become a reality. We have had children of prisoners serve as counselors, grandmothers teaching the girls to cook and sew, and mechanics teaching the boys how to change oil. We have had campers share their pain with a counselor and find hope in Christ. Each year we have seen middle class young adults pouring out their lives to bring hope to children of prisoners.

The dream is expensive. It costs time, money, and comfort. But none of us would trade the entire world for the treasure of seeing others find joy and hope in Christ.

I'd like to invite you to ask God how you can be part of His dream. You won't be disappointed."

Will you ask God how you can be part of His dream?

Appendix A.

A Tale of Pearls·

Ben wrote this poem/story for one of our Banquets' for Hope, and several staff girls acted it out as it was read. I thought you might enjoy reading about some of our pearls at camp...

It is Monday morning, sometime in late June.
Camp staff are all working, to be ready by noon.

There are three acres of grass, all being mowed by Zack.
While wranglers groom horses, and clean up their tack.

Jen ate and left early, with the St. Louis bus,
The trip without a bouncer counselor, would be disastrous.

In the Pearl's wagon, stuffed animals were set out by Kate.
Faith straightened a quilt, as for their campers they did wait.

There was a gift for each girl, a stuffed animal and backpack;
Inside was a Bible, a flashlight, and what else they might lack.

When everything was set out, in its very own place,
They bowed their heads in prayer, and asked God for grace.

It was about mid-afternoon, when giggling in came the team.
To shy little Yunis, the gifts all seemed like a dream.

"This wagon is too cool," said Sonya, one of the tough tomboys,
While Tia and Destiny traded hair clips, and talked about boys.

Then looking at Faith, Destiny asked with great interest,
"How many babies do you have? Tell me about them, I insist."

"Children?" said Kate, "I'm only 18, and I've not yet been wed!
"What has that to do with babies?" said Destiny, scratching her head.

After a short discussion on the purpose of families, marriage, and all,
They headed for field games, and then to supper in the dining hall.

That night after showers, came each girl with her flashlight,
Ready for bed – when they saw the most disturbing sight!

There was a moth, a daddy long leg, and even a spider!!
And there fearlessly stood, shy Yunis, with everyone behind her!

Was little Yunis afraid? Why certainly not!
With her small little cage, each insect she caught!

Yet the battle raged on as each moth came by flight,
Until they finally won – when they turned out the light!

As they settled into their beds laughing to each other,
Yunis talked about the bugs' cage, and then it slipped, "My MOTHER!"

In an instant, like a blanket, there fell such a hush,
Through dark, and silence, each girl felt her blush.

After a moment, that had the weight of eternity,
"My dad's in for life," somberly spoke Destiny.

Next shared Sonya, all sad and forlorn,
"My mom was in prison, since the day I was born"

Then it was Tia, who snarled it out.
"My dad's in prison, I hope he never gets out."

It was homeschooled Faith, who was next to speak,
With a broken heart, with a tear stained cheek;

"I don't know your pain, and I can't tell you why,
But it's wounds like these, that make God cry."

Kate prayed a simple prayer, and then said, "Sleep tight",
And the only sounds now, were the sounds of the night.

They lay there in silence, being washed of their shame,
Like dusty flowers, in a nice gentle rain.

It was 6 am, when Yunis did rise,
With a bushy tail and bright brown eyes.

Try as she might, the others to wake,
until taken out, by counselor Kate.

The rest woke, by Faith's force,
Just in time, for the obstacle course.

Though everyone was there, and they started on time,
The five minute course, took them more than nine.

Each girl was mad, at the other's faults she had seen,
The problem was clear; they needed to work as a team.

After a skit on forgiveness, and camp songs had been sung,
They all memorized a verse, and Commandment number one.

Next on orange juice, pancakes, and sausages did they dine,
While Tia ate ½ a pancake, Sonya ate nine.

Back in their wagons, after the Bible was read,
Destiny asked Kate a question, and then dropped her head.

"What do you do when, you know you are bad?
I have tried really hard, but I still feel mad!"

Kate shared about God, and the gift He has given.
How if we trust in Jesus, all our sins are forgiven.

It was later that day, Destiny did her part,
She started following Jesus, and gave Him her heart.

Next came the horses, games, archery and crafts.
All but Tia played like children, complete with deep belly laughs!

Tia said it was stupid, and she hated it all,
For with each of her hurts, she'd built a protective wall.

The week marched on, to Thursday night,
They sang around a fire, and warmed in its light.

The Awards Time, had finally come,
Time for certificates, for what the girls had done.

The Pearls were first, on this special occasion,
Destiny received one for Diligence and Determination.

Next was Yunis, for Bravery and Joy;
And they told how she'd captured each bug like a boy!

Sonya's was for Encouragement and the story they did tell,
Was how on the Obstacle Course, "You go girls!" she'd yell.

Her second was for Courage, in an interesting way,
For she wore her first dress, on the Princess Dinner day.

Hardened Tia, was last for this activity,
Her award required all her counselor's creativity.

The first was easy, she was Orderly they did find.
The second was for Honesty, she always spoke her mind.

After sharing a story, of how they knew this was true,
They called her up, gave her a hug, and said "We love you."

Though you couldn't hear it, and she played her tough girl part,
A once firmly placed brick, fell from the wall in her heart."

"Our Favorites "Library

For those interested, we have included a list of some of our favorite books that have inspired and changed us on our journey.

Rogue Angel by Jodi Werhanowicz
Hope Rising by Kim Meeder
Kisses From Katie by Katie Davis
A Cry From the Streets by Jeannette Lukasse
Lillian Trasher by Janet & Geoff Benge
Climbing by Rosiland Goforth
George Muller by Janet & Geoff Benge
Too Small to Ignore by Dr. Wess Stafford
GOSPEL by J.D. Greear
The Good and Beautiful God by James Bryan Smith
The Power of a Whisper by Bill Hybels
Helping People Win at Work by Ken Blanchard
Family Arrested by Ann Edenfield
Ax-i-om by: Bill Hybels (Powerful Leadership Proverbs)
Leading On Empty by Wayne Cordeiro
Do Hard Things by Alex & Brett
9 Things You Simply MUST DO by Dr. Henry Cloud
Boundaries by Henry Cloud and John Townsend
Quiet Leadership by David Rock
One Thousand Gifts by: Ann Voskamp
Capture His Heart (or Her Heart) by Lysa TerKeurst
The DNA of Relationships for Couples by Dr. Greg Smalley and
                                   Dr. Bob Paul

Recommended Resource:
Angel Tree: www.prisonfellowship.org

Join our Camp David Family!

Please contact us or visit our website! We would love to send you our email updates, and quarterly newsletters.

Camp David of the Ozarks

P.O. Box 1607

Rolla, MO 65401

cdo@campdavidozarks.org

www.campdavidozarks.org

Use this QR CODE to go to our website and make an online donation, or find out how you can be part of the Camp David Ministry.